IMAGES
of America

ALDERWOOD
MANOR

IMAGES
of America

ALDERWOOD MANOR

Marie Little, Kevin K. Stadler, and the
Alderwood Manor Heritage Association

ARCADIA
PUBLISHING

Published by Arcadia Publishing
Charleston, South Carolina

Library of Congress Catalog Card Number: 2006936024

For all general information contact Arcadia Publishing at:
Telephone 843-853-2070
Fax 843-853-0044
E-mail sales@arcadiapublishing.com
For customer service and orders:
Toll-Free 1-888-313-2665

Visit us on the Internet at www.arcadiapublishing.com

CONTENTS

ACKNOWLEDGMENTS

The authors wish to thank the Port Gamble Museum for providing images for this book, as well as access to the Pope and Talbot Archives, which contain a great deal of historical information on the community of Alderwood Manor. We appreciate the University of Washington, Museum of History and Industry, South Snohomish County Museum, and the City of Lynnwood, who have allowed us to include photographs from their collections. We are also grateful to Dale Hoggins, who wrote papers while a student at Edmonds High School and the University of Washington, thereby providing valuable historical information for this book.

Many individuals have helped to establish dates and identify people or places. In cases where our sources were not certain of identifying information, we have indicated an approximate date or left pictured individuals unidentified.

Our sincerest gratitude goes out to the membership of the Alderwood Manor Heritage Association for the photographs and stories they continue to provide and, more importantly, for their passion for the community.

INTRODUCTION

The planned community of Alderwood Manor was developed in 1917, halfway between Seattle and Everett. Before 1910, when an electric trolley line running from Seattle to Halls Lake was extended to Everett, only a few hardy pioneering families lived in this remote central part of South Snohomish County. A trip to Seattle took two days along a route following the long-abandoned "telegraph trail," which was cut through the forests for a cable system intended to link North America with Asia and Europe through the Bering Sea. At Edmonds, transportation to Seattle continued by boat or by train.

The interurban cut travel time to Seattle to about an hour. Completion of the rail corridor also opened up the opportunity for the Puget Mill Company to develop 7,000 acres of timberland. Logging operations had converted acres of forest to a land of blackened stumps and snags, but this nonproductive land was taxed at the same rate as timberlands, and the Puget Mill Company began selling off portions of their logged-off land as "stump farms."

As a key element in a real estate promotion referred to as the Alderwood Manor Plan, the company developed a poultry farm on 30 acres east of the interurban tracks. Here, purchasers of 5- and 10-acre tracts were taught to raise poultry for profit and vegetables to feed their families. A two-story hotel and a community hall were built for the benefit of the community.

Just across the tracks, 10 acres were set aside as urban lots. A brick, Tudor-style general store and a two-room model school were built to serve the growing community. As the Puget Mill Company developed their land marketing scheme, the people who had come to live on the land developed a community. Soon, a Sunday school and a Masonic lodge were organized. By January 1921, the small model school had been replaced by a new brick building. The Puget Mill Company remodeled the old schoolhouse into an office that included four spaces available for leasing to local businesses.

Meanwhile, a couple of miles west, paving had begun on the new Pacific Highway. Crews worked northward from the King County line and southward from the Everett city limits, until they met at the intersection of the present 164th Street Southwest. In October 1927, a ribbon-cutting ceremony opened the highway to traffic. Keeler's Korner, a mom-and-pop grocery store/gas station, was built on the southeast corner of the intersection. Soon it was joined by other highway related businesses—more service stations, auto courts, and roadhouses.

In 1931, a road (now 196th Street Southwest) was paved to connect Alderwood Manor to the new highway. For a decade, the highway corridor and the rail corridor complemented one another. In 1934, the community turned out to celebrate the opening of a two-and-one-half-mile section of paved road west of Highway 99, joining Alderwood Manor to Edmonds. The intersection where the new road crossed Highway 99 became known as the Alderwood Crossroad.

Meanwhile, back at the demonstration farm, the effects of the Great Depression were being felt. The Puget Mill Company closed the demonstration farm, leasing the central five acres to

Norm Collins, who established the Washington Breeders Hatchery. The remaining 25 acres were subdivided into one-acre "ranchettes" in 1935, and even the community hall was remodeled and sold as a residence.

Back at the Alderwood Crossroad, a Seattle realtor platted acreage on the east side of Highway 99, naming it "Lynn" for his wife, and "wood" for the Alderwood District to the east. Soon businesses located at the crossroad adopted the name Lynnwood, and a business district developed, while Alderwood Manor developed as a suburban residential community.

As automobiles became the favored mode of transportation, fewer people rode the interurban. The line was abandoned in 1939, and merchants moved from the old Alderwood Manor Town Center to the new Lynnwood Business District.

Development slowed with the onset of World War II. Building materials were difficult to come by, and the focus of the community was on working for the war effort.

After the war was over, many stump ranchers, who had barely survived during the Depression, paid off their mortgages and owned their land free and clear. This, coupled with a housing shortage in Seattle, brought about a demand for suburban property. Even unused chicken houses became assets because they could be quickly remodeled into rentals.

Population continued to explode from Seattle into South Snohomish County. Traffic increased on Highway 99, leading to the installation of a traffic light at the Alderwood Crossroad in 1948. Streets were renumbered from the Everett city limits to the King County line, and the Alderwood Crossroad became the intersection of 196th Street Southwest, and Highway 99.

Lynnwood incorporated as a city in 1959, with its eastern boundary about a mile west of the Alderwood Town Center. Some residents were concerned that their rural lifestyle was being threatened. Not only was Lynnwood encroaching on their territory from the west; construction of a freeway was advancing from the east.

The former community hall lay directly in the path of the freeway. It was sold and moved to a site on the southeast corner of the what was previously the demonstration farm. The Alderwood Road was widened for better freeway access, and businesses on the south side of 196th Street Southwest were demolished and rebuilt farther back from the street. The old brick Tudor Alderwood Mercantile, although stripped of its veranda-style entrance, was left standing. Eventually it was sold to an appliance repair business. As freeway construction continued, the remnant of the demonstration farm was further isolated from the old Alderwood Town Center, and few people were aware of the once famous demonstration farm's existence.

An election to incorporate Alderwood Manor in the 1960s failed, and the town center was annexed into Lynnwood a couple of years later. In 1978, the Alderwood Mall was built on the old Morrice homestead, and in the early 1990s construction of a new freeway interchange at 196th Street Southwest was planned. The remains of the demonstration farm, including the water tower and the superintendent's cottage, were discovered, still standing, on the original location east of the freeway, with an entrance off Poplar Way.

Although the land where the demonstration farm once stood is buried beneath the freeway, tourists can now visit Heritage Park, located halfway between Seattle and Everett at I-5's Exit 181-B, and see historic structures from the rural community of Alderwood Manor, preserved in the city of Lynnwood.

One

EARLY DAYS

HUNTER CABIN. Duncan Hunter, originally of Aberdeen, Scotland, built this cabin in 1891 on his 80-acre homestead in the forested hills about 10 miles east of Edmonds, Washington. His wife, Jennie, and sons William and Gordon waited in Wisconsin to join him. Pictured here several years later are Duncan, Gordon, Jennie, Reuben, Basil, and William. Perhaps their clothesline was a discarded wire from the old telegraph trail.

WILLIAM MORRICE FAMILY. Duncan Hunter encouraged his friend to move to a 100-acre homestead adjoining his. William purchased it in his wife's name in 1893. Elizabeth, Jennie Hunter's sister, brought their three children and her mother to live there until her husband could join them—some three years later. Ruth, Jessie, William Jr., Elizabeth, and William are pictured here after the family was well established in the community.

MORRICE CABIN. When William, who had been working as a stone mason in the east, joined his family in 1896, he built this sturdy cabin and cleared land for an orchard. Their daughter Ruby died at age 10. Ruth, the youngest, was born on the homestead.

HUNTER HOME AND MORRICE ORCHARD. The two-story frame house on the hill was built in 1914. Jessie Morrice married James Hunter, Duncan's nephew, who worked on the house as a carpenter. Logging operations have converted the enormous trees that surrounded the Hunter cabin into tall, barren stumps. The orchard on the Morrice farm is visible in the foreground. The narrow road pictured between the two farms became the north branch of North Trunk Road and is now Thirty-sixth Avenue West. Telephone poles sprouted soon after 1910, when electricity became available with the extension of the electric-powered interurban trolley line to Everett.

EARLY POSTCARD OF HALLS LAKE. In 1908, pioneers including the Burlesons, the Salties, and the Lambes were just beginning to divide their claims and sell acreage in the Cedar Valley community near Halls Lake, which was the end of the line for the interurban. This lake can still be seen north of present-day 212th Street Southwest, and west of Forty-fourth Avenue West in Lynnwood.

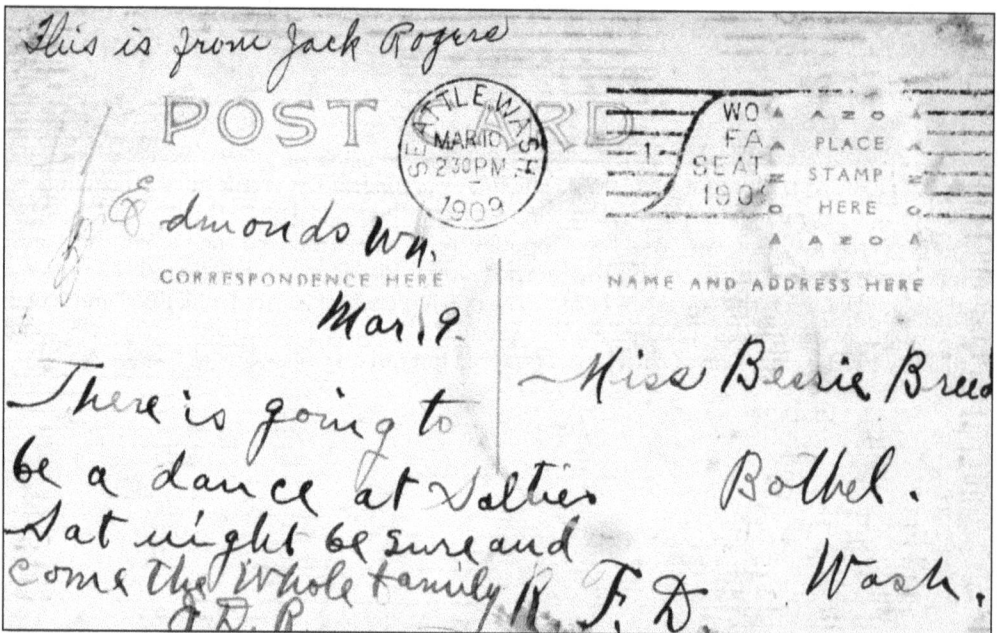

EARLY POSTCARD MESSAGE. The front of this postcard, mailed in 1909, shows Halls Lake. The Breed family would have traveled over five miles from their home at Martha Lake to the dance at the Salties. The following year, they could have made the trip in minutes on the interurban, but they would have had to leave by 10 p.m.

OLD SETTLERS PICNIC. In the Gay Nineties, the Burlesons and several neighbors gathered for a picnic to celebrate a birthday. This became an annual event, and for more than 100 years, descendents of South Snohomish County pioneers have gathered for the Old Settlers picnic at an Edmonds park in August. Pictured here in the 1970s are Jennie Hunter, Charles Breed, and Grace Burleson at an Old Settlers Picnic.

BROWN'S BAY LOGGING COMPANY, C. 1902. Charles P. Crary stands on a springboard, while two loggers sit on the undercut to sharpen their axes. Note that the falling saw, used for making the undercut, is propped up against the trunk of the fir tree being cut. Crary, Charles Breed's brother-in-law, was a timber cruiser for Brown's Bay.

LOGGING NEAR FUTURE SITE OF ALDERWOOD MANOR. Donkey engines like the one working at left in this photograph were used to haul the enormous logs to a landing where they could be loaded onto a steam locomotive to Puget Sound. Once they were made into log booms, they were floated to mills in Seattle. This image of logging in South Snohomish County was captured in 1910 by Darius Kinsey, who documented the logging industry in the western United States from 1890 to 1925. Note how small the men appear next to the immense logs. The exact location pictured is not clear, but it is probably about halfway between Seattle and Everett, near I-5 Exit 181.

DONKEY ENGINE. By the turn of the century, donkey engines, such as this one pictured setting on skids, replaced the teams of horses that dragged the logs into place earlier. Also pictured are an unidentified logger and timber cruiser Charles P. Crary. Cruisers were employed to survey trees for quality and density and plan the quickest and cheapest way to harvest the timber.

BROWN'S BAY LOGGING CREW. The same locomotives used to haul logs were also used to transport loggers to and from work. The logging railroads were not stationary; tracks were taken up and moved from one location to another as logging in the area progressed from one stand of timber to another, c. 1910.

16

INTERURBAN APPROACHING MARTHA LAKE. The land on both the left and right was owned by Samuel McGhee, who moved from Tennessee to the 160-acre homestead in 1886. The interurban tracks cut the McGhee property in half. Note the pile of timber on the right. McGhee sold some of the timber he cut as railroad ties. Later he acted as a guide for hunters who rode the interurban out from Seattle to hunt ducks at Martha Lake. (Courtesy University of Washington Special Collections, Puget Power #353.)

WAITING FOR THE INTERURBAN. This may be the only photograph ever taken at the Forest Park Interurban stop, which was halfway between Seattle and Everett. No one knows the lady's name or when the picture was taken. She was photographed between 1910, when the interurban rail line was extended from Halls Lake to Everett, and 1917, when the name of the stop was changed to Alderwood Manor.

ALDERWOOD MANOR STATION, C. 1920. In 1917, the Puget Mill Company platted Alderwood Manor No. 1, and Forest Park became Alderwood Manor. The brick Tudor building was the Main Store, built in 1919 to serve the growing community.

SEATTLE AND EVERETT INTERURBAN LINE. This map from a 1925 timetable of the Pacific Northwest Traction Company shows an interurban line running from Seattle to Bellingham. While the Seattle–Everett line had operated successfully since 1910, the line from Bellingham extended only to Mount Vernon. The Bellingham–Everett line was never completed. The two lines were known as the Northern and Southern Divisions of the Pacific Northwest Traction Company. The map shows stage (bus) connections to towns not served by the electric trolleys, and there was an interurban line between Everett and Snohomish, and between Mount Vernon and Sedro Woolley.

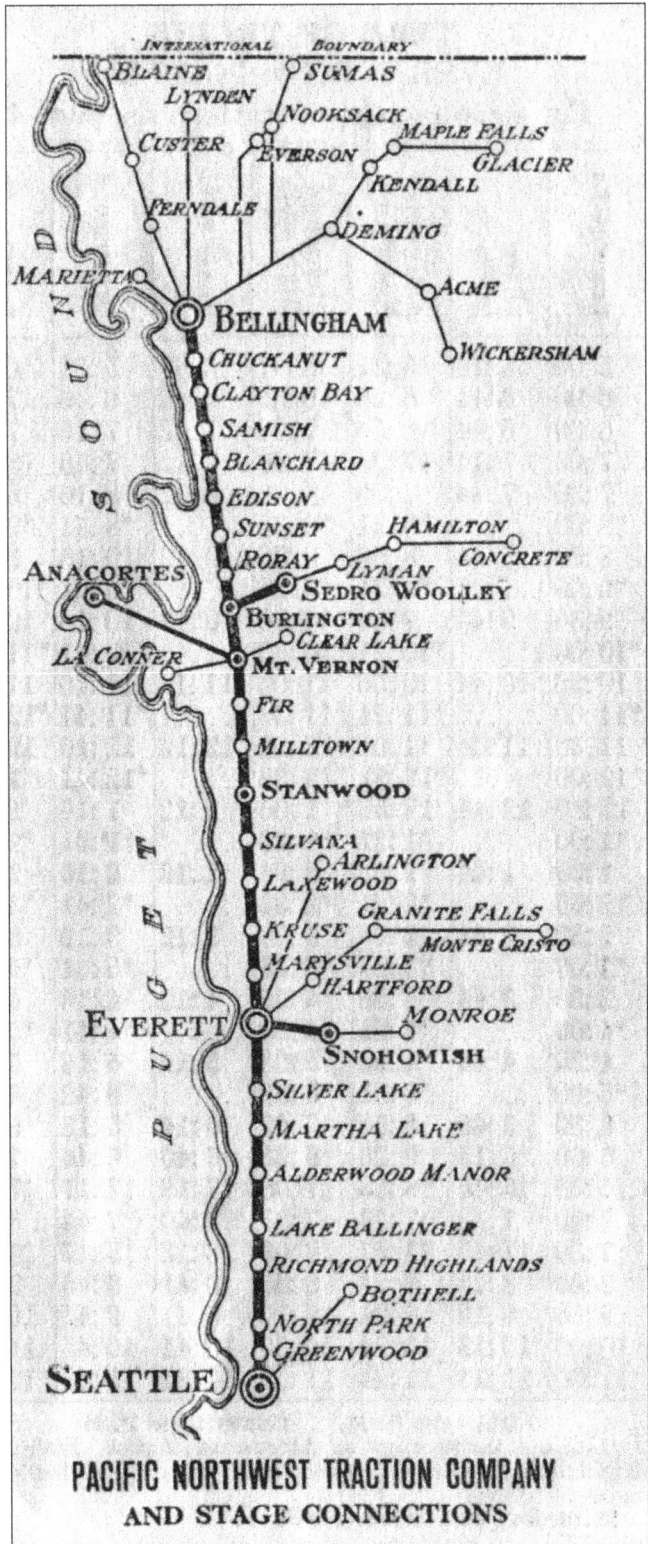

INTERNATIONAL BOUNDARY

BLAINE — SUMAS
LYNDEN
NOOKSACK
CUSTER — MAPLE FALLS
EVERSON — GLACIER
KENDALL
FERNDALE
DEMING
MARIETTA — ACME
BELLINGHAM
CHUCKANUT — WICKERSHAM
CLAYTON BAY
SAMISH
BLANCHARD
EDISON
SUNSET — HAMILTON
RORAY — CONCRETE
ANACORTES — LYMAN
SEDRO WOOLLEY
BURLINGTON
LA CONNER — CLEAR LAKE
MT. VERNON
FIR
MILLTOWN
STANWOOD
SILVANA
ARLINGTON
LAKEWOOD
GRANITE FALLS
KRUSE — MONTE CRISTO
MARYSVILLE
HARTFORD
EVERETT — MONROE
SNOHOMISH
SILVER LAKE
MARTHA LAKE
ALDERWOOD MANOR
LAKE BALLINGER
RICHMOND HIGHLANDS
BOTHELL
NORTH PARK
GREENWOOD
SEATTLE

PUGET SOUND

PACIFIC NORTHWEST TRACTION COMPANY
AND STAGE CONNECTIONS

LAST DAYS FOR THE INTERURBAN. Interurban Car No. 55 is pictured here at Alderwood Manor in 1939. A woman at left waits to board for a ride to Everett. The building behind the tiny Alderwood Manor Depot is the Washington Poultry Association (commonly known as The Co-op). The water tower is on the grounds of the Alderwood Grade School, which is the brick building on the far right.

CAR 55 EN ROUTE TO EVERETT. A close look at this photograph reveals that the woman in the above photograph has just boarded. The brick building on the right is the Puget Mill Company's Main Store, which became the Alderwood Mercantile in 1933. In 1939, all these buildings stood on land that was eventually cleared for the freeway interchange at 196th Street Southwest and Interstate 5.

LAST FREIGHT CAR. Freight was hauled mostly at night. Various agricultural products, including berries, cherries, nuts, eggs, and even live baby chicks were shipped out. Supplies such as feed, coal, and parts for farm implements were delivered. The last freight car to leave the line was the Northern Pacific boxcar, parked by the Washington Cooperative Farmers Association building. The brick Tudor Alderwood Mercantile is visible on the right.

BREAKDOWN AT MARTHA LAKE. A little more than a week before the last trip, Car 53, looking the worse for wear, has broken down just north of the Martha Lake Station. The conductor is holding the car momentarily before signaling the motorman on Car 55 to move south. Note changes around the Martha Lake Station since the photograph on page 17 was taken—shortly after the first trip in 1910.

ABANDONED IN THE WOODS. After 30 years of service on the Seattle–Everett Interurban line, Car 55 moved to Everett and spent 20 years as a diner on Highway 99. In the early 1960s, the car moved to Snoqualmie and served as a ticket booth for the Snoqualmie Valley Railroad Museum for a while. Car 55 remained in the woods, waiting to be rescued, until 1996.

ABANDONED RIGHT-OF-WAY. Even the tracks were removed soon after the trolleys ceased running. Some 50 years later, the old track route was resurrected as the Interurban Trail, and today it is used by bicyclists and pedestrians. Approximately 75 percent of the original right-of-way still exists. Interstate 5 has taken up the remaining 25 percent.

Two

THE ALDERWOOD MANOR PLAN

DEMONSTRATION FARM COTTAGE AND WATER TOWER. These structures occupied the central 5 acres of the 30-acre farm developed by the Puget Mill Company in 1918. The cottage was lit with electric lights, and the water tower was equipped with an electric pump, thanks to the nearby electric trolley line. The cottage was built as a residence for the superintendent of the farm.

"For the Individual, a Little Land and Liberty;
For the Community, Co-Operation and Efficiency."

NEW LIFE OF THE LAND. Reproduced here and on the facing page are the front and back panels of an early marketing brochure produced by the Puget Mill Company. The pamphlet unfolds, like a road map, to an illustrated newspaper article explaining the meaning of the Alderwood Manor Plan. It was defined as "a plan for the intensive use of five acres of land for poultry raising for egg production and for providing vegetables for the family table for winter and summer use,

THE HOPE OF THE LITTLE LANDS

That Individual Independence shall be achieved by Millions of Men and Women, Walking in the Sunshine without Fear of Want.

That in response to the Loving Labor of their Own Hands the Earth Shall Answer their Prayer —"Give us this Day our Daily Bread."

That they and their Children shall be Proprietors rather than Tenants, working not for Others but for Themselves.

That theirs shall be the Life of the Open—the Open Sky and the Open Heart— Fragrant with the Breath of Flowers—More Fragrant with the Spirit of Fellowship which makes the Good of One the Concern of All and Raises the Individual by raising the Mass.

— W. E. Smythe

"THE NEW LIFE OF THE LAND"

ALDERWOOD MANOR

with a supplementary income from fruits, berries, nuts and other agricultural products." Of course, the heart of the Alderwood Manor Plan was the $250,000 the demonstration farm, designed to teach the art of making a living from five acres of land. One illustration is "a Social Hall on the Demonstration Farm Grounds, where entertainments, musicales and lectures upon varied subjects may be held through the winter season." (Courtesy Port Gamble Museum.)

VIEW OF THE DEMONSTRATION FARM FROM INTERURBAN. The community hall, which was used for lectures on agriculture as well as for community events, is just beyond the fence to the left. In back of the hall, and partially hidden, is the hotel which had an incubator house in the basement. The superintendent's cottage and the water tower are visible on a knoll at the center of the farm. The other buildings are chicken houses. People from across the country came by train to Seattle then rode the interurban to Alderwood Manor to see the demonstration farm, proclaimed by Prof. James Rice of Cornell University to be the finest anywhere.

COMMUNITY HALL SHORTLY BEFORE OPENING OF FARM. This view looks north at the entrance of the community hall. Just beyond the chicken houses north of the hall is the road that is now 196th Street Southwest Just beyond the fence on the left is the Alderwood Manor Station. A portion of the hotel is visible on the right. (Courtesy University of Washington Special Collections, #9455.)

INTERIOR OF INCUBATOR HOUSE. The incubator house, in the basement of the steam-heated hotel, had a capacity of 55,000 day-old chicks per hatch and four or five hatches in a season.

Aldewood Manor
Aug 10-1921

AMERICAN POULTRY ASSOCIATION CONVENTION. Alderwood Manor was recognized by the American Poultry Association as one of the country's greatest poultry centers, when delegates to the organization's annual convention visited this community and held one of their sessions here in August 1921. Here delegates are pictured touring the demonstration farm. (Courtesy University of Washington Special Collections, #UW 25819.)

INTERIOR OF LAYING HOUSE. Chickens were bred for high egg yield. Workers were aided in monitoring and recording the production of each hen by these "trap nests," which held the chicken and egg captive until each egg was counted.

EGGS PRODUCED BY WORLD CHAMPION HEN. This photograph appeared in marketing brochures produced by the Puget Mill Company to entice people to come to Alderwood Manor, raise chickens, and become rich. The 326 eggs arranged on the bottom of a wash tub graphically illustrate the number of eggs laid in one year by world champion hen Babe Ruth.

"BABE RUTH"
World's Champion Layer
Record 326 eggs in a year
Bred and raised at :—
Alderwood Manor

52

WORLD-FAMOUS BABE RUTH. This portrait is of world champion egg layer Babe Ruth. She was named for the famous home run champion ball player because she had a home run (laid an egg) nearly every day for a year. The hen's vital statistics have been carefully recorded and attached to her photograph.

PUGET MILL GRANARY. This large granary was built to store feed and supplies bought in carload lots at wholesale prices for resale to poultry farmers below retail prices. When Norm Collins leased the farm in 1933, the Puget Mill Company reserved half of the warehouse for their own use, and Collins set up a modern hatchery to replace the existing obsolete equipment. In 1943, he built a new hatchery on the foundation of the old granary. (Courtesy University of Washington Special Collections, #UW 25818.)

LADY WITH CORNSTALK. This photograph of an unidentified woman was probably taken at a fair held at the Alderwood Manor demonstration farm, either in 1920 or 1921. The event, financed by stock sales to Alderwood Manor residents, gave people an opportunity to show their products and helped advertise land for sale. (Courtesy University of Washington Special Collections, #UW14730.)

DEMONSTRATION FARM GARDEN. Fred Musiel was employed as a nurseryman and gardener on the demonstration farm. He tended this model garden, which produced $550 worth of vegetables in 1919. Later, he established his own business, the Alderwood Manor Gardens, and sold berries and other nursery stock to the farmers.

FEEDING CHICKENS. On the demonstration farm, chickens weren't confined as they are today. These hens had the run of a cherry orchard outside the long row of laying sheds. F. C. McClane, who was superintendent of the farm from 1920 to 1933, is pictured here feeding some of the hens.

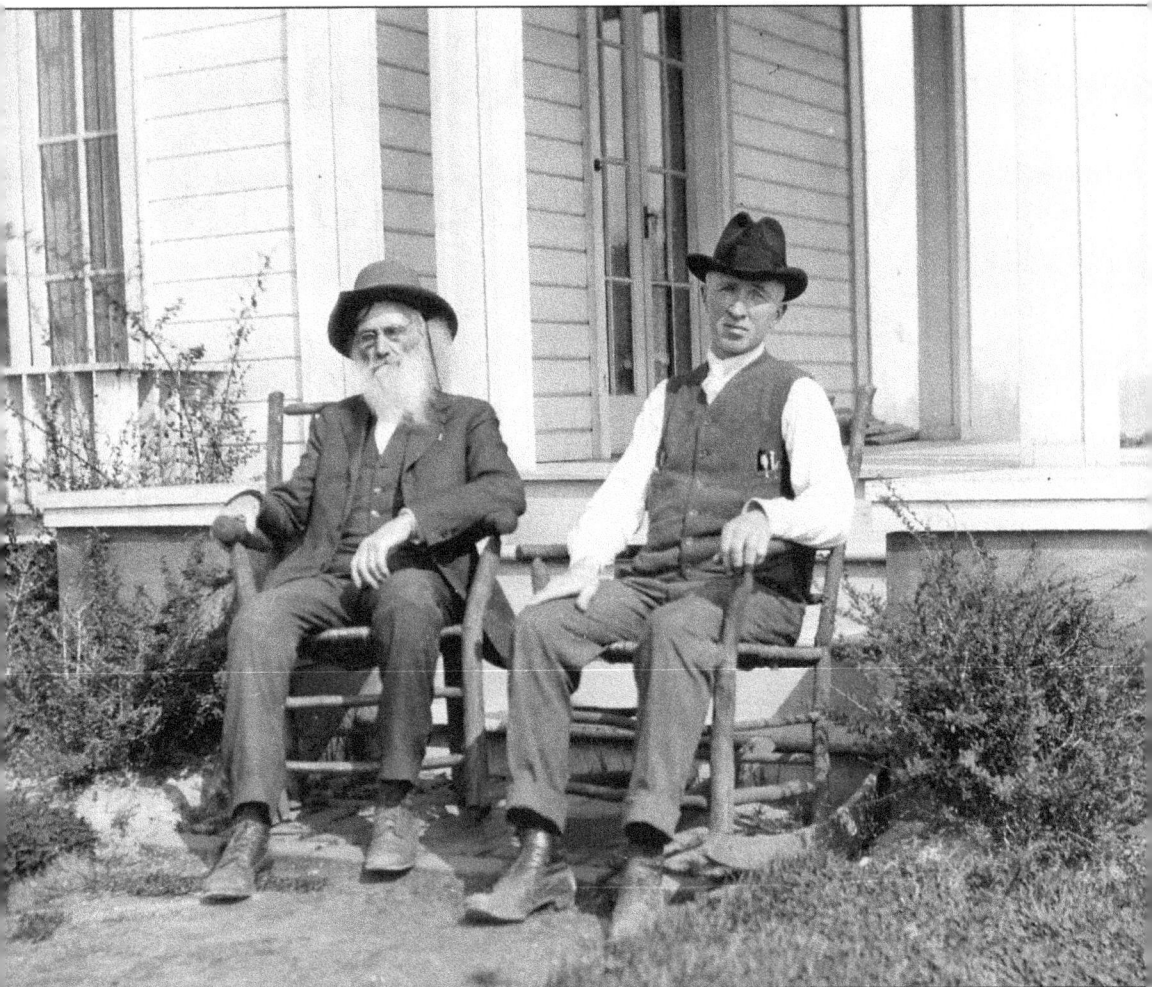

VISITING THE DEMONSTRATION FARM. Ezra Meeker was a pioneer who came across the Oregon Trail to Washington Territory in 1852, settling in the Puyallup Valley. He wrote books about the Oregon Trail and traveled it several times—by wagon, touring car, and by airplane in 1924 at age 93. Here he is seated on the left, next to F. C. McClane, in front of the superintendent's cottage, c. 1920.

Single Comb White Leghorns

Feeding and Care *of* the Commercial Flock

By F. C. M^cCLANE

Superintendent of the

ALDERWOOD MANOR
DEMONSTRATION FARM

Alderwood Manor, Washington

CONTENTS

BROODING AND CARE OF BABY CHICKS
FEEDING AND CARE OF THE COMMERCIAL FLOCK
DETAIL PLAN OF TRAP NESTS
DETAIL PLAN OF FORCE ROOST
IMPORTANT GENERAL INFORMATION

PRICE 50 CENTS

POULTRY RAISING MANUAL, 1922. This reproduction of the cover of a poultry raising manual written by F. C. McClane indicates the professional quality of the instructional materials that were provided for Alderwood Manor chicken farmers. The classes were designed for people to learn by doing. Each day, something different was taught, until all the fundamentals of the chicken business had been covered. The courses usually lasted two weeks and cost about $200. A free, six-week course was also offered once a year. McClane visited those who were operating their own poultry farms and offered advice to anyone who asked for it.

WASHINGTON COOPERATIVE FARMERS ASSOCIATION. Mr. McClane, is among the members of Board of Trustees and management executives photographed in 1923, (front row) Frank J. Swayne, H. J. Karcher, Carl Laakso, Oscar H. Swanson, and W.H. North; (back row) F.C. McClane, Sales Manager H.E. Wills, President S.D. Sanders, Comptroller D.S. McDole, R.T. Hawley, George H. Griffith and George W. Holt.

WESTERN FARMERS ASSOCIATION BUILDING. The association, under a new name, continued to provide egg and poultry marketing services and farm supplies to its members. In 1927, this modern four-story plant with full basement and office was built at 201 Elliott Avenue West in Seattle.

SUCCESSOR TO THE DEMONSTRATION FARM. The Alderwood Manor Plan and the demonstration farm became casualties of the Great Depression. In the early 1930s, the demonstration farm was closed and leased to Norm Collins who established Washington Breeders Hatchery in buildings on the central five acres. In 1935, the remainder of the farm was subdivided as one-acre "ranchettes." Even the Social Hall was remodeled and sold as a residence.

CHICK WAGON DELIVERY TRUCK. Norm Collins and his staff posed in front of one of the Washington Breeders' "Chick Wagon" delivery trucks which covered all of Western Washington. Pictured, from left to right, are (first row) Alice Ludden, Margaret Richardson, and Honey McNeil; (second row) Norm Collins, William Sutin, George Tanabe, Tracy McNeil, and William Schmiedeke.

Poultry Guide

By NORMAN COLLINS

Manager the Alderwood Manor
Demonstration Farm, and the
Washington Breeders' Ass'n, of
Alderwood Manor, Washington.

•

Best Modern Brooding Methods

How to Raise Healthy Pullets

How to Manage Laying Hens

including proven feeding schedules
for maximum egg production

Disease Control

including Coccidiossis, Paralysis,
Leukemia, and other recent and little
understood mortality causes.

●

A Complete and Strictly Practical Manual for the
Commercial Poultryman

Price 50 cents

POULTRY RAISING GUIDE, 1938. Nearly 35 years after F.C. McClane wrote a manual to instruct both amateur and professional poultrymen in the "art" of raising poultry, Norm Collins wrote this "complete and strictly practical" manual directed to commercial poultrymen. By the time Collins arrived on the farm, the state of the art equipment installed 25 years earlier was obsolete, while poultry raising methods had kept pace with the development of modern technology. The model farm had been operated for 16 years primarily for real estate promotion and community service. Collins needed to run it as a profitable business, and he did so for 37 years.

MODEL FARM. This model house was adjacent to the demonstration garden (see page 32). After the demonstration farm was closed, it was sold to the Hudson family. Several families purchased their water from the water tower perched atop a tall stump. Later, Norm Collins moved the house from Poplar and Filbert (today's 196th Street Southwest) to his hatchery property to house some of his employees. (Courtesy University of Washington Special Collections, #UW 18420.)

EGG PRODUCTION. Edward Gyldenfeldt, originally of Denmark, moved to Alderwood Manor in 1920. He is pictured here with his wife, Jenny, next to the house he built on their five-acre farm. This photograph illustrated many of Puget Mill's marketing pieces. (Courtesy Port Gamble Museum.)

ALDERWOOD MANOR'S MAIN STORE. The Puget Mill Company built this store to serve the growing community in 1919. In 1920, residents petitioned for a post office and mail came in on the interurban. Note that snags and stumps are all that remain of the tall evergreens that once surrounded the former Forest Park Station. (Courtesy Port Gamble Museum.)

REAL ESTATE OFFICE MOVES TO TOWN CENTER. In 1922, the model school was moved onto a foundation closer to the road and remodeled as a modern brick store. In this *c.* 1935 photograph, the space at the south end is occupied by Puget Mill Company offices, and the four store fronts are rented to businesses that include a barbershop and the post office.

FUTURE SITE OF POULTRY FARM. Although Puget Mill cleared one acre on each of the five-acre home sites, the farmer frequently had to deal with large rocks as they improved their land. Even today, in many suburban housing developments one can still see huge rocks incorporated into the landscaping.

LOOKING NORTH FROM TOWN CENTER. The Alderwood Manor Model School is on the left. Note that houses have been built on both sides of the North Trunk North Road (now Thirty-sixth Avenue West). This road runs northward beyond the Hunter and Morrice places (see page 11). (Courtesy University of Washington Special Collections, #UW 14392.)

HOME ON ALDERWOOD MANOR CHICKEN FARM. This home was probably built by the Puget Mill Company. Note the shingle siding, which may have come from the shingle mill on Halls Lake in Cedar Valley, so named for the dense groves of cedar trees that grew there.

ONE OF THE LARGER HOMES AT ALDERWOOD MANOR. Note the attached well house on the right. Most housewives had to walk outside to pump water for cooking and bathing, and not all pumps were covered by a well house. Illustrations of this house were frequently used in promotional materials. It was demolished in the 1990s and replaced by a basketball court in Lynnwood's Spruce Neighborhood Park.

FIRE LOOKOUT TOWER. Jim Daniel, fire warden for the Puget Mill Company, stands atop the tower he built at the present intersection of Thirty-sixth Avenue West and 164th Street Southwest. The Daniel family lived in Meadowdale, near Puget Sound, several miles west of Alderwood Manor. During the summer months, however, he would move to Alderwood Manor with his wife, Muriel, and their two daughters. One time when Jim was out fighting a fire, a runaway fire started near here. Muriel left their baby with a woman who lived nearby, warning her to "take the baby and run, if the fire gets away from us and starts to come up the hill." She then rounded up some old men, and they got some shovels and started a back fire, saving many Puget Mill homes in the area.

Three

SCHOOL DAYS

HUNTER SCHOOL. The first schoolhouse in Alderwood Manor was built on the northwest corner of the Hunter Homestead in 1895. There was no school property in the Alderwood Manor District, but when the Edmonds School Board was petitioned to provide a school, they voted to "leave the matter with parties living in the area." Mr. Hunter had built a log cabin, and the board voted to pay him $1.60 per day to fix it up. The district furnished two yards of blackboard cloth. Children from the Breed, McGee, Hunter, and Morrice families attended the school.

Edmonds

Public

Schools

Report of *Reuben Hunter,*

for year 1900.

J. A. Stiger.
Teacher

GRAMMAR AND HIGH SCHOOL

Month — Arithmetic, Drawing, Geography, Grammar, History, Language, Music, Spelling, Reading, Physiology, Writing, Algebra, Rhetoric, Composition, General Average, Days Present, Days Absent, Times Tardy, Deportment, General Average

Principal

HUNTER BOYS' REPORT CARDS. These century-old report cards were discovered at a garage sale and donated to the Alderwood Manor Heritage Association archives. Reuben Hunter's report card (above) was signed by J. A. Stiger in 1900, the first year he taught at the Hunter School. Stiger was paid a salary of $45 per month for an eight-month term. William Hunter's report card was signed by Alewisa Kennedy, who taught at the school for only one term in 1898.

Teacher's Monthly and Term Report Card.

Report of *William Hunter* a pupil of the *Hunter* School.

PARENTS ARE REQUESTED TO EXAMINE THIS CARD CAREFULLY AND TO VISIT US.

189_ Month	Arithmetic	Drawing	Geography	Grammar	History	Language	Music	Spelling	Reading	Physiology	Writing	Algebra	Rhetoric	Composition	General Average	Days Present	Days Absent	Times Tardy	Deportment	General Average	PARENT'S SIGNATURE
1																					Hunter
2																					Hunter
3																					Hunter
4																					Hunter
5																					
Avg's.																					

Explanation:—100 signifies Perfect; 85 Good; 75 Medium; 50 Poor; 25 Unsatisfactory.

TO PARENTS AND GUARDIANS: Parents and Guardians will find it greatly to the interest of the pupil to see that it has no tardy or absentee marks. Systematic and constant effort will be made to interest pupils and to stimulate them to thorough and diligent exercise of their intellectual and moral faculties. Your co-operation will greatly aid in making the work successful.

October 14 189_ *Alewisa Kennedy* Teacher.

OLD SCHOOL AND NEW SCHOOL. The two-room model school was moved onto a new foundation closer to the present Thirty-sixth Avenue West, and remodeled (see page 39). The old school still stood in 2005, while the new school was demolished in 1992. Note the false front on the building across the street (now 196th Street Southwest) from the new school.

ALDERWOOD ELEMENTARY SCHOOL. Although it was named the W. A. Irwin School, it was generally referred to as the Alderwood Grade School, as pictured here c. 1940. After the school closed in 1963, the building was used as the administration building for Edmonds School District 15. In 2005, the Lynnwood Convention Center was built across 196th Street Southwest from the former school site. (Courtesy Edmonds–South Snohomish County Historical Society.)

45

DEDICATION OF NEW SCHOOL. Speakers at a dedication ceremony pictured here include W. A. Irwin, for whom the school was named; Stiger, the prosecuting attorney for Snohomish County who had taught at the Hunter School; Albert Chase; and other school board members. The gentleman on the left may be Mr. Irwin.

FIRST GRADUATING CLASS OF NEW ALDERWOOD SCHOOL. Fourteen eighth-graders graduated in 1922. Pictured, from left to right, are (first row) Beatrice Norgaard, Bothell; Donizella Read, Alderwood Manor; Helen Grant, Bothell; Helen Faivre, Alderwood Manor; Mary Stodeick, Edmonds; Dorothy Newcomb, Edmonds, and Margaret Newcomb, Edmonds; (second row) Bernard Coyne, Bothell; Orville Rudd, Alderwood Manor; Harry Chapman, Alderwood Manor; Harold Chase, Alderwood Manor; Curtis Peterson, Alderwood Manor; Martin Swartz, Edmonds, and Charles Hutter, Alderwood Manor. (Courtesy Edmonds–South Snohomish County Historical Society.)

STAFF OF ALDERWOOD SCHOOL. Seated in front of the school in 1936 are the teachers, administrators, and custodian. Pictured, from left to right, are (first row) Mae Delameter, Eula Stallings, ? Caspers, Blowden Enoch, Loretta McSorley, Mildred Hatch, Jenny Beebe (principal), Dorothy Moe, Ethel Faulkerson, and unidentified; (back row) Mr. Engler (custodian), Mr. Osborn, Thomas Tucker, and Julius Dornblat.

TEACHER'S RETIREMENT LUNCHEON. Teachers gathered at a luncheon on the occasion of Miss Delameter's retirement, c. 1942. Pictured, from left to right, are Mrs. Stallings, Mrs. Fulkerson, Mrs. Bird, Miss Nolton, Mrs. Denby, Mrs. Beebe (principal), and Miss Enoch; (standing) Miss Delameter, Mrs. Allen, Mr. Allen, Mrs. Burke, Mrs. Salisbury and her son George, Mr. Burke, unidentified, and Harold Nelson.

TRANSPORTING STUDENTS TO SCHOOL. In the 1920s, some students rode the interurban to the Alderwood Manor Grade School. The insert above right may be the Yost Motor Company bus, which carried Alderwood students to Edmonds High School. Leo Echelbarger and Earl Martin, owners of Alderwood Auto Freight, outfitted a truck with benches and contracted to bus children to the Alderwood Grade School for $375 per month. This image dates to approximately 1926.

SCHOOL BUS FLEET, MID-1930s. In the mid-1930s, new "Mac Bulldog" buses were purchased, and by 1940 there were seven buses in operation. A garage for bus maintenance was built northeast of the Alderwood Grade School. Here the bus center left is entering the garage, and three other buses are parked. The water tower on the school grounds was removed shortly after this picture was taken.

SNOHOMISH COUNTY BASKETBALL CHAMPIONS. Alderwood Grade School's champs lined up in front of the school for this 1942 photograph. Pictured, from left to right, are (first row) Warren Little, Loyd Twede, ? Russell, Wylie Echelbarger, and Keith Schonor; (second row) Loren Stewart, Scott Schultz, Jack Eisen, Larry Engler, Jack VanNortwick, Pete Hoff, Bill Ewing, and Coach Jack Allen.

GIRLS BASKETBALL TEAMS. These sixth-, seventh-, and eighth-grade players of 1941–1942 are, from left to right, (first row) Rita Schimmel, Dorothy Stadler, Delores Lee, Barbara Cambell, Astrid Ellingson, and Betty Beck; (second row) Mary Lou Jones, Jean Brampton*, Mary Lou Carter, Harriet Skutvick*, Drusilla Thompson, and Betty Denby*; (third row) Lorna Wilcox, Patsy Peterson, Pat Procter*, Joan Peterson*, Ardell Wilcox*, and Eythel Salisbury. (* = first team)

FIRST JUNIOR HIGH SCHOOL IN DISTRICT. After World War II, enrollment in the three District 15 grade schools increased, requiring operation on double shifts. In 1948, the Lynnwood Community Club donated 10 acres located near the intersection of Highway 99 and 196th Street Southwest, and an adjoining five acres was purchased for Lynnwood Junior High School, which opened in 1954. (Courtesy Edmonds–South Snohomish County Historical Society.)

EDMONDS HIGH SCHOOL AUDITORIUM. Alderwood Manor students attended Edmonds High School from 1920 to 1957, when a new Edmonds High School was opened on 212th Street Southwest and Seventy-sixth Avenue West. Pictured is the auditorium that was built in 1937 and renovated as a performing arts center in 2005–2006. On the far left is the original (c. 1900) brick building, which was demolished in 2005.

Four

COMMUNITY GROWTH

TENDING CHICKENS ON GYLDENFELDT FARM. This farm was on Beech Road near the interurban line (visible on the upper right), pictured *c.* 1920. From left to right are Flo Christianson (holding baby), Jenny Gyldenfeldt (wearing a hat), and an unidentified woman. Freeway construction in the 1960s obliterated this site, which is now east of Forty-fourth Avenue West, near I-5 exit 181-A.

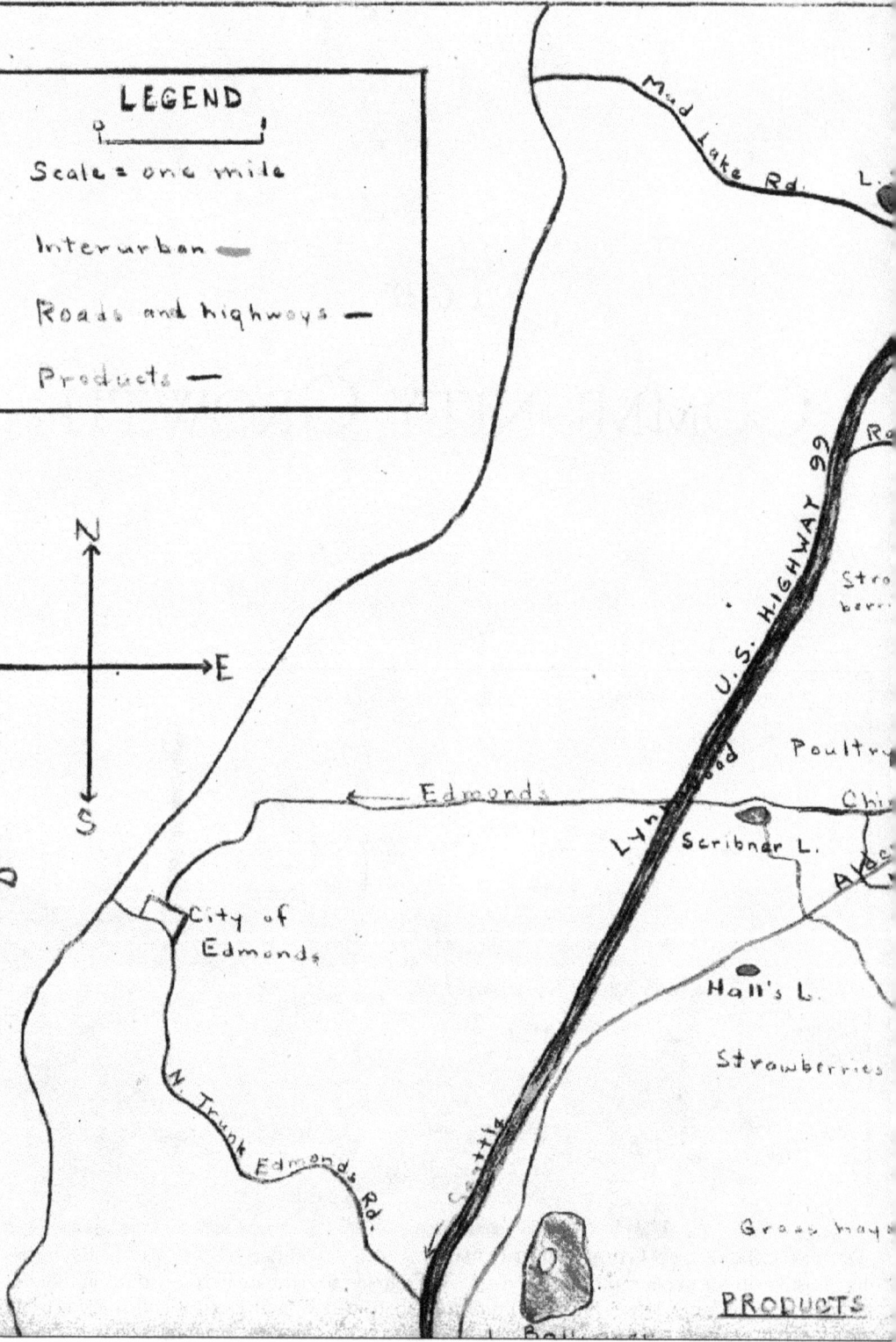

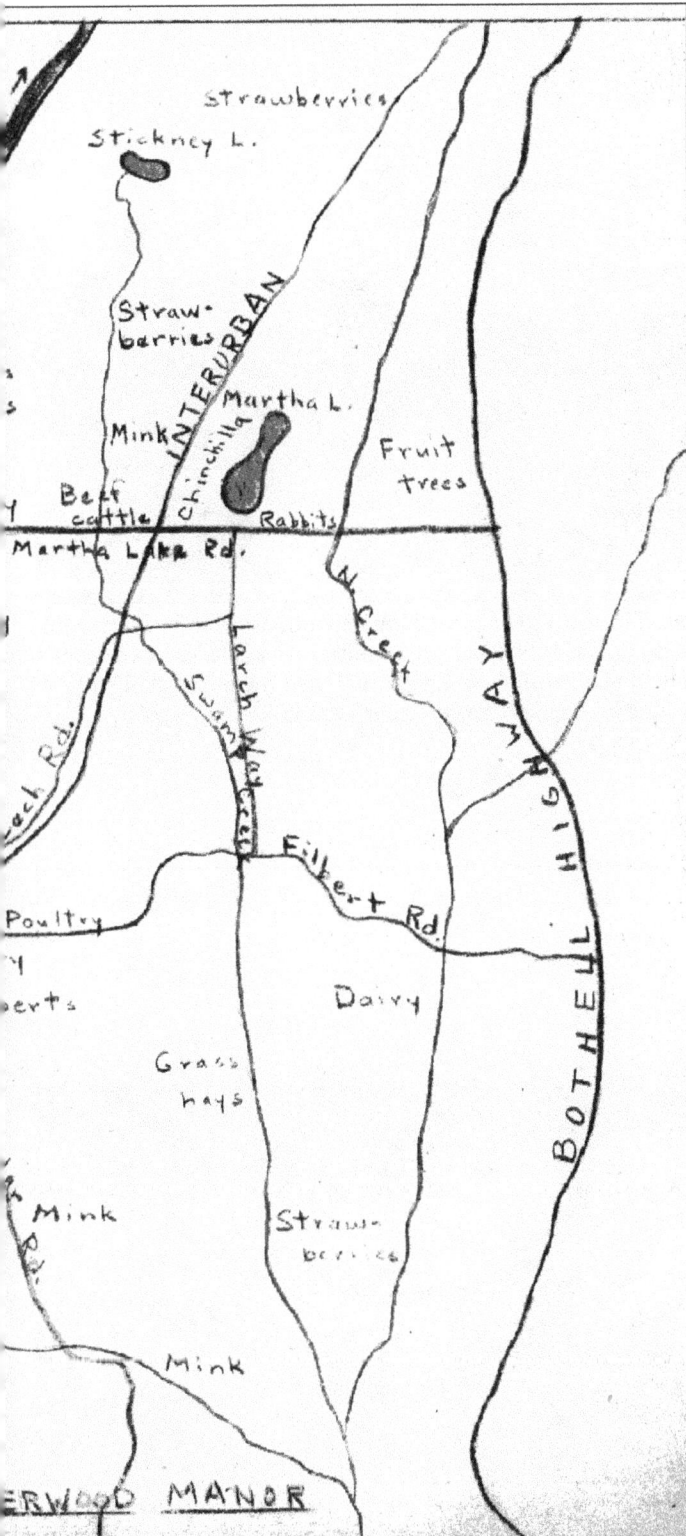

ALDERWOOD MANOR.
This map was drawn by Dale Hoggins to illustrate a history of Alderwood Manor prepared for his senior English course at Edmonds High School in the spring of 1950. It indicates the route of the interurban, Highway 99, and the principal roads built by the Puget Mill Company about 1918. Martha Lake Road is now 164th Street Southwest, and Filbert Road still exists, but somewhere west of Swamp Creek it becomes 196th Street Southwest. Note Mud Lake Road, which follows a westerly route, past Lake Serene, from Highway 99. Mud Lake was renamed Lake Serene when the area was subdivided, and it was believed that no one would pay a good price for waterfront property on a lake named "Mud."

FAMILY WORKING ON FARMHOUSE. This family has moved into their house built by Puget Mill. The chicken house on the right is also finished. Two men are working on a ladder propped against the porch. Perhaps the women are contemplating how long it will take them to pick up all the rocks so a garden can be planted. This photograph was taken around 1920.

SMALL FARMHOUSE AND GARDEN. Many couples moved into two-room houses, like this one pictured c. 1920, and added rooms as their families grew with their gardens and poultry flocks.

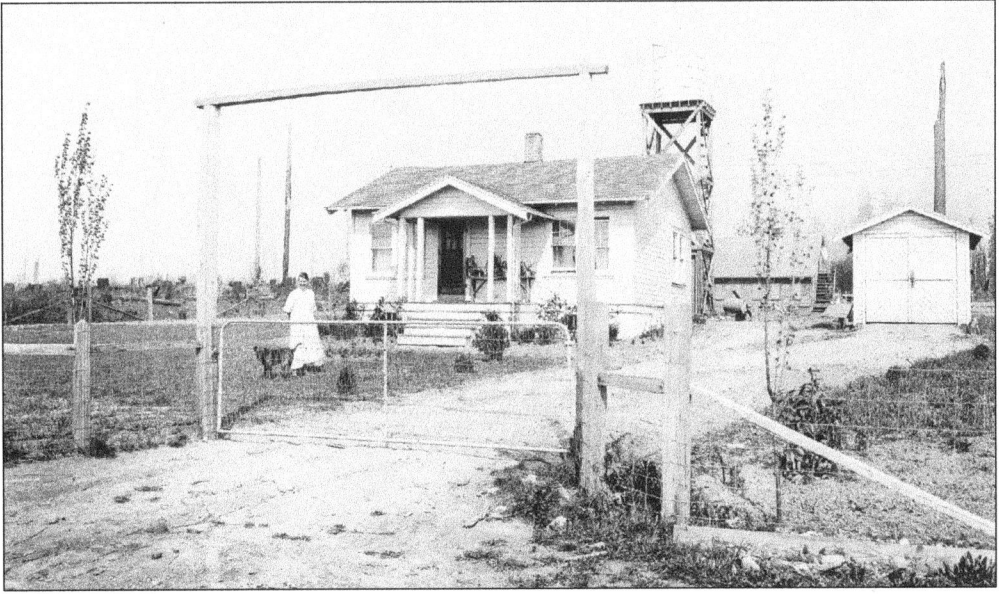

WOMAN IN FRONT OF FARMHOUSE. This family, photographed around 1920, appears to be well established on their farm. The wife often was responsible for much of the farm work, because few families could survive on the income from their farms. To support their families, the men would often commute to jobs in Seattle, Everett, or other places near the interurban line.

WATER TOWER ON MORRICE RANCH. The size of this water tower, pictured c. 1900, can be estimated by noting how small the people working on it appear in comparison. An unusual feature of the Morrices' water tower was the windmill, which provided power to operate the pump.

CHASE AND ECHELBARGER FAMILY PICNIC. Albert and Grace Chase moved to Alderwood Manor from North Dakota in 1917, seeking better educational opportunities for their daughters. Their daughter Helen had come out west to attend the University of Washington and married an Alderwood Manor boy named Leo Echelbarger. The couple raised their nine children in a house that still stands on the corner of 188th Street Southwest and Fortieth Avenue West.

WILCOX CHILDREN AT SCRIBER LAKE, 1928. Looking east, telephone poles mark the location of the Alderwood Road, now 196th Street Southwest. The Wilcox house overlooked the lake, where the children swam, fished, and built a fleet of rafts. They played, trapped mink, and hunted quail and pheasant on the shore. Pictured, from left to right, are Harold, Lorraine, Ken (seated), Elsworth (Al), and Eugene Jr.

ALDERWOOD WATER DISTRICT GROUNDBREAKING. The southeast corner of 164th Street Southwest and Thirteenth Avenue West, pictured here, is now occupied by a bank. Peter Tutmark, chairman of the board of water commissioners turned the first spade of dirt here for a $350,000 water project in 1933. Seated center front, on a seat that was removed from a car for the occasion, is pioneer Elizabeth Morrice. Other dignitaries pictured include two county commissioners and the president of the Everett Chamber of Commerce. On June 15, 1934, the Everett Chamber of Commerce led an auto caravan to Alderwood Manor, where a carnival, complete with fireworks, was held on the school grounds to celebrate the completion of the project.

STENBOL FAMILY'S MODEL T. Around 1924, Helen and Laura Stenbol and a friend are pictured beside North Trunk Road, now Thirty-sixth Avenue West. (Courtesy Edmonds–South Snohomish County Historical Society.)

AERIAL VIEW OF MAPLE ROAD HOUSE. The Conklin House at the upper right was built on the northwest corner of North Trunk Road and Maple (the diagonal road) in 1917. Pictured here in the 1950s, it still stands as an historic centerpiece to a development of affordable homes built in the 1990s by the Housing Authority of Snohomish County. The snow-covered fields on both sides of Maple are now covered with houses.

HORSE RANCH ON THIRTY-SIXTH AVENUE WEST. South of the Conklin House on the east side of Thirty-sixth Avenue West sat this picturesque farm where, by 1950, chicken farming was abandoned for horse raising. Now the grassy knoll has been leveled for another housing development.

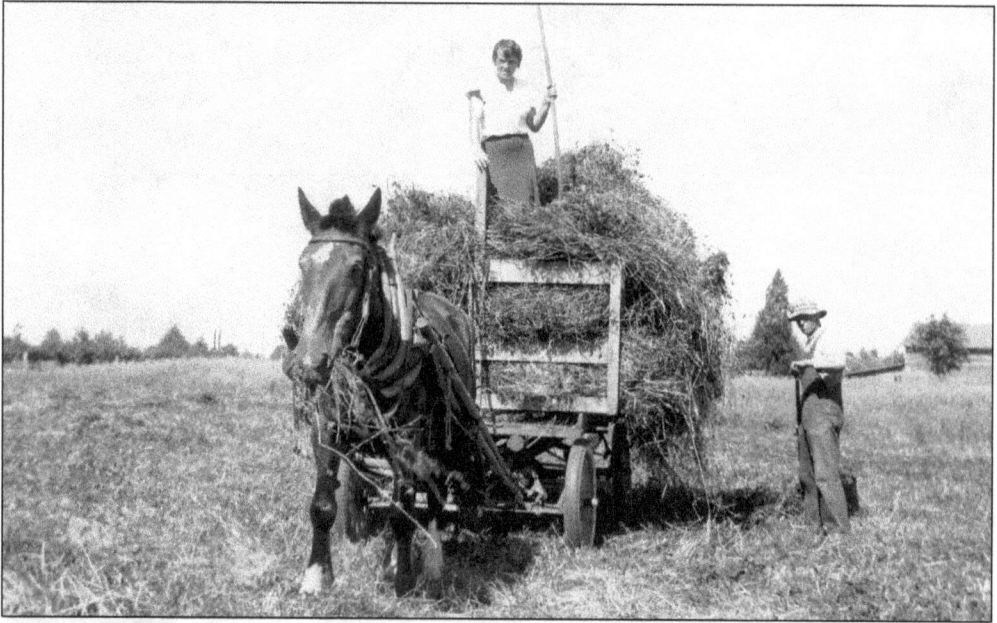

HAYING ON STENBOL FARM. Hay cut on this farm, located on the North Trunk Road in 1924, was fed to work horses and the family cow. Lorentz Stenbol still lived at 155th and Thirty-sixth Avenue West in 1962, and was listed as a farm worker in the local directory. However, farms were becoming smaller as they were being subdivided into suburban home sites. (Courtesy Edmonds–South Snohomish County Historical Society.)

TUTMARK HILL HOUSE. Andrew Tutmark built this home on his chicken farm located on Maple Road, east of the interurban right-of-way. Five brothers from Minnesota bought farms on the hill that later was dubbed Tutmark Hill. They later raised mink instead of chickens. Andrew and Marie's house was demolished in the 1990s and replaced by a housing development named English Hill. The Peter Tutmark house still stands.

SMITH STRAWBERRY FARM. When Clarence Smith purchased a chicken farm on Cedar Way (now Forty-fourth Avenue West), it bordered the interurban tracks. By the time he had replaced chickens with strawberries, the property was adjacent to an I-5 Freeway entrance ramp. Now the Lynnwood Park and Ride Lot has replaced the strawberry field.

POULTRY AND TURKEY FARM. The Hewett's farm was on Larch Way, southwest of the Alderwood Town Center, c. 1935. In addition to their chickens, which they kept for egg production, they raised turkeys and chickens for sale at a farmers market in West Seattle.

THOMSON FAMILY. Jean Thomson Holt used this big stump as a backdrop for a photograph of her younger brothers and sisters in 1929. Pictured, from front to back, are Elbert, Val, Myrle, Bob, Barney, and Phyllis. Jean recalls that the stump was across Martha Lake Road, north of their place, which was on Manor Way. Now Martha Lake Road is 164th Street Southwest and Manor Way is a parkway that leads directly to the Alderwood Mall. (Courtesy Edmonds–South Snohomish County Historical Society.)

EMILY WILLIAMS PICKING BERRIES. About half a mile east on Martha Lake Road, Emily Williams pauses by a stump on their property shortly after she and her husband, Lew, moved to Alderwood Manor, c. 1920.

STUMP ON JAMES AND ALICE LITTLE'S PLACE. The Littles purchased land on Cedar Way (now Forty-fourth Avenue West), about two miles northwest of Alderwood Manor. Standing on the stump, *c.* 1920, from left to right, are (first row) Gladys Deming, ? Miller, Grace Deming, and Ralph Deming; (second row) two Miller boys and De Ette Miller; (at base of stump) Mildred Little Deming (the Littles' daughter), Wilma Miller (the Littles' niece), Alice Braymon Little, and James Little. The size of the stump can be estimated from James's height—six feet, two inches.

EASTER EGG HUNT AT CHURCH. By 1940, the Alderwood Community Church east of the Masonic temple sponsored many community events.

SWIMMING IN CEMENT POND. Wouldn't Beate Gyldenfeldt and her friends be surprised to learn that their neighbors' swimming pool had been converted to Lynnwood's Park and Ride? This pool was on the Bevier place, across the road from the Gyldenfeldts. Some old-timers remember Mrs. Bevier teaching them to swim.

BIRTHDAY PARTY AT LOBDELL PLACE. Halide (on the right) celebrated her birthday, with friends, in the backyard of their home in 1931. This is now the site of a Jack-in-the-Box drive-through restaurant on the northeast corner of Forty-fourth Avenue West and 196th Street Southwest in Lynnwood.

VIEW OF LAKE SERENE. The Williams family moved from their home on Martha Lake Road to a residence on the north side of Lake Serene. Young Bob Williams paddles his canoe toward their house in this picture that looks southwest. The white building on the left is the Langdalen's boathouse, c. 1940.

ICE SKATING ON LAKE SERENE. It was so cold in the winter of 1949 that Bob's younger brother, Jack went ice skating in front of the family home on Lake Serene.

LEW WILLIAMS TILLING GARDEN. Lew Williams tills the garden at his home on Martha Lake Road in the 1920s. He bought the property in Alderwood Manor after serving in World War I and commuted to work at the Ford Motor plant in Seattle until it closed. He also worked for the Puget Mill Company, painting the houses they owned, c. 1925.

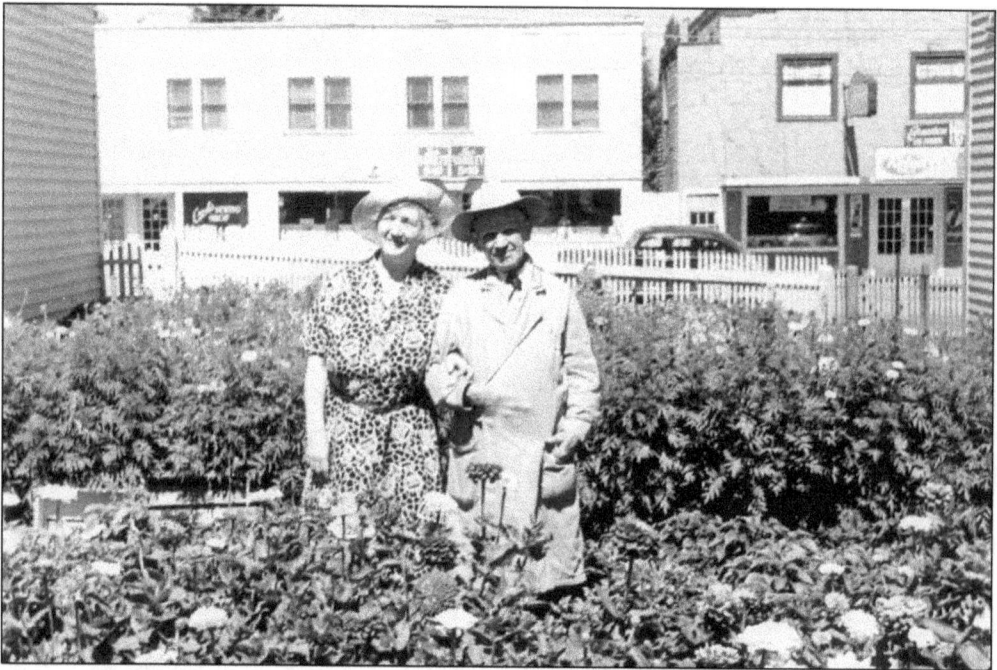

DAHLIA GARDEN IN DOWNTOWN ALDERWOOD. Pictured here are Mr. and Mrs. David Dahlin in their dahlia garden, located on a lot between their Red and White Store and Alderwood Drugs on the south side of 196th Street Southwest. Note that all of the stores across the street have living quarters on the second floor.

JACK BENNETT'S CHICKEN FARM ON NORTH TRUNK ROAD NORTH. Jack Bennett bought this poultry farm, a quarter of a mile south of the Martha Lake Road in 1938, and raised fryers for five years. He and his wife, Hazel, then moved closer to the Lynnwood Business District, where they owned a tavern for several years. Eventually he set up a real estate business and was elected the first mayor of Lynnwood in 1959.

FROM EGGS TO FURS. Just as the Puget Mill Company closed the demonstration farm and went into real estate sales, many Alderwood Manor chicken farmers moved from the egg business into the fur business. Some farmers started fox farms, but most went into raising mink because the small animals required about the same space as chickens. Dawson's Chinchilla Ranch was located north of 164th Street Southwest on Meadow Road (Thirteenth Avenue West). Most chinchillas were raised as breeding stock rather than for pelts.

EARLY MINK RANCH. One of the earliest mink ranches and also one of the last to close was the Smith's. The sheds in the foreground are breeding pens, and the pens on the right are pelting pens, where the young, born in May, are raised from July or August until the pelts are harvested in November. Robert and Elizabeth Smith moved from Alaska to Alderwood Manor in 1936 and purchased a 10-acre chicken farm on Larch Way South, near Poplar. They bought mink that had been trapped on Kodiak Island, building sheds with material salvaged from the chicken houses on their farm. In 1952, their son Rod returned from service in the Marines and took over the business. Rod and his cousin Clarence Corbin operated the ranch until 1972.

Facts About

INCORPORATION

Alderwood Manor is growing up. The adoption of incorporation as a third class city is the first step in bringing Alderwood Manor to the front as a growing, progressive, efficiently operated city. Don't let Alderwood Manor, and yourself as a taxpayer, down. The adoption of incorporation for this area means good government for all of us here.

Incorporation is not new! It is a step in natural growth. Our own people are given a greater voice in writing their own laws by ordinance, rather than having them dictated by the county. ☙ It is democratic! The council is elected by the people and can be recalled by the people! All its meetings and actions must be public, when all interested citizens can attend and voice their objections, if any.

The facts listed below are submitted for your consideration, when you go to the polls on March 29.

By being an incorporated city, the community has an agency through which it can express itself, meet its problems with first hand knowledge of its local area, and supply necessary services to the extent desired to satisfy local needs and as financially feasible.

Incorporation is a tool for building an integrated and unified local government, with additional powers for self-determination of local affairs (municipal home rule).

A city may provide better fire and police protection.

A city may regulate traffic, speed limits, and may control hazards.

Streets can be operated, repaired and maintained better.

Cities are entitled to about $12 per capita of state-collected, locally shared taxes (gasoline tax, motor vehicle excise tax, and liquor profits and taxes).

Other sources of city revenue include 15 mills from the property tax, business and occupation taxes, fines and penalties, permits and license fees, and franchise fees and payments.

ABOUT TAXES: We are already paying the taxes mentioned. The only question involved is whether we want to continue to let the county spend this money of ours, or whether we think we are capable of spending this money ourselves through local government. Incorporation will not cost us more money in taxes. By law the tax take of a city is limited to 15 mills.

———————————————

CITY OFFICERS TO BE ELECTED MARCH 29

Mayor: Ted Moffett, Clarence Sievert; **City Clerk:** Kay Thaler, Charley Embree; **City Treasurer:** Alice Miller, Anna M. Wilson.

City Council (seven to be elected): Harold Dykeman, George Thorleifson, Virgil Schoentrup, Floyd Eller, Kenneth Wilcox, Leonard Spry, Edward Eschrich, Walter Lancaster, Richard Hays, Gordon Bowers, William Grote, Robert Farrar, Jarvis Border.

SHOULD ALDERWOOD MANOR INCORPORATE? Lynnwood had been an incorporated city for nearly a year when the residents of Alderwood Manor went to the polls to decide whether they should also become a city. Although the proponents presented a strong case, voters decided that Alderwood Manor should remain a rural community. A few years later, property owners in the vicinity of the town center petitioned to be annexed to Lynnwood because street lights, sewers, and police protection were provided within the city limits.

Five

ALDERWOOD MERCHANTS

FREIGHT BUSINESS BEGAN. In the early 1920s, Leo Echelbarger bought the Alderwood-Seattle Express and hauled fuel, including wood, coal from Issaquah, and freight from Seattle and Everett to Alderwood. In partnership with Earl Martin, under the name Alderwood Auto Freight, some of the trucks were outfitted with benches to transport students from East Alderwood, Mud Lake, and Cedar Valley to the Alderwood School. In 1935, the partnership dissolved. Martin specialized in hauling wood and coal, while Echelbarger delivered oil in addition to freight. In 1946, Echelbarger's company merged with Edmonds Auto Freight to become Edmonds-Alderwood Auto Freight.

TOWN CENTER, 1929. A photographer captured this panoramic view just over a decade after the community of Alderwood Manor emerged, halfway between Seattle and Everett. The Alderwood Town Center already boasts a three-story building—the Masonic temple on the far left. The one-story structure across the street is the old model school that the Puget Mill Company has remodeled into an office for their real estate division with four retail spaces, one of which is leased to a barber. The water tower over the well in back of the building provides water to several nearby

residences. The hotel on the hill just to the right of the water tower is on the demonstration farm. The superintendent's cottage and the social hall are to the right of the hotel. The brick Tudor Main Store faces the street. It is now owned by Guy and Hannah Parker and has been named Parker's Store. The new Alderwood Manor School is the large building farthest to the right, and the long building in between is the Alderwood Plant of the Western Farmers Association. (Courtesy Museum of History and Industry.)

ALDERWOOD CONSTRUCTION AND HARDWARE COMPANY. This close-up view of the back of the Puget Mill Real Estate building shows the Alderwood Construction and Hardware building across the street. The small square building between the real estate building and the hotel is probably the new telephone exchange, and the long building to the left is probably a warehouse for Alderwood Construction Company.

DAVID DAHLIN MOVES DOWNTOWN. When David Dahlin built this new grocery store in the town center on the south side of the present 196th Street Southwest, his brother Arvid continued to operate their original store on Martha Lake Road a couple of miles north. Although Parker's Store was just a block east, there were enough customers for everyone, and the atmosphere was one of cooperation rather than competition. This photograph was taken c. 1940.

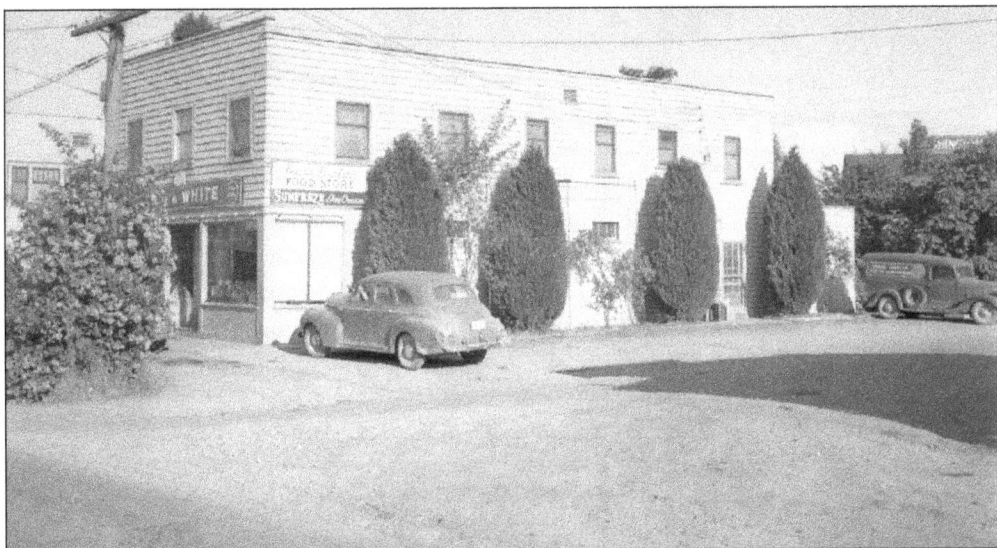

ANOTHER VIEW OF RED AND WHITE STORE. This view, looking east, shows the living quarters above the store Dahlin built in 1930. Typically the merchants in Alderwood lived upstairs. Even though some later had a residence nearby, it was often convenient to have a place to cook a meal or put the children to bed for a nap.

RED AND WHITE STORE DELIVERED. A phone call to "2272" was all that was required to receive a home delivery of groceries from Alderwood Food Center. The little boy peeking out from the truck window is most likely the Dahlins' son Carl David.

INTERIOR OF ALDERWOOD FOOD CENTER. Pictured is Bill Birt, who came to work in the store a couple of years after it opened and moved into the apartment upstairs. The Birts bought the store from the Dahlins in 1955 and operated it as Birt's Food Center until the building succumbed to a bulldozer in 1964. It was a victim of a street improvement project that widened Alderwood Manor's two-lane "Main Street" to accommodate increased traffic to I-5, already under construction.

INTERIOR OF ALDERWOOD MERCANTILE. Herman Wickers and his sales staff were standing ready to serve their customers when this photograph was taken in the late 1930s. Pictured, from left to right, are Wickers, Ted Neiderhauser, and Ed Schoenholz. Ed started working at the store soon after graduating from Edmonds High School in 1935.

76

LOOKING EAST FROM TOWN CENTER. This photograph, taken by Carl David Dahlin in 1952, is looking east on Alderwood Road (196th Street Southwest). H. J. Wickers pumps gas at the Alderwood Mercantile on the right.

HORSES WAITING FOR RIDERS. It was not unusual to see young members of the Pegasus Patrol riding their horses to Alderwood in the 1950s. These horses are hitched up just across the road from the Alderwood Mercantile. Two of a row of poplar trees that grew along Poplar Way are visible on the right. Poplar was the eastern boundary of the old demonstration farm.

MRS. SEAVY'S DRY GOODS AND NOTIONS. Mrs. Seavy's store was in the north bay of the Post Office Building on North Trunk (now Thirty-sixth Avenue West). Pictured, from left to right, are Laura Seavy, Gene Haworth, unidentified, and Merle Haworth. Note the wood-burning heating stove in the right-hand corner, c. 1935.

EVERGREEN DECORATORS. The first issue of the *Evergreen Empire News* announced that Lew C. Williams and Clyde C. Randall would open a home decorating business on January 6, 1934. The store was located in the Post Office Building, the first door north of the Alderwood Manor Post Office. Note the evergreen logo on top of the finial on the left. The newspaper office was located in the same building.

EVERGREEN DECORATORS MOVES. In the 1940s, Evergreen Decorators moved across the street into the building that had once been the Alderwood Construction and hardware store. Note that they have expanded and are now selling appliances in addition to paint, window shades, draperies, and linoleum.

WELL-STOCKED SHELVES. Lew Silver bought the Post Office Building in 1947, and moved his family into the former Puget Mill Real Estate offices, which had been remodeled as an apartment. He started a hardware store in the three adjoining spaces, and even though the space on the north was rented to postmaster Ed Schoenholz, the building is called Manor Hardware to this day.

FIRE ENGINE STANDING READY. The International fire truck purchased in 1946 is parked on the north side of 196th Street Southwest, in front of Norm Johnson's barbershop, c. 1950. There are three storefronts in this building that Norm built in the early 1930s.

VARIETY STORE ON NORTHEAST CORNER. In the 1950s, Annabel Lee bought the building from Norm Johnson. She was a widow and hoped it would provide income to raise her two sons. She operated a variety store in two of the storefronts and lived in the upstairs apartment with her boys.

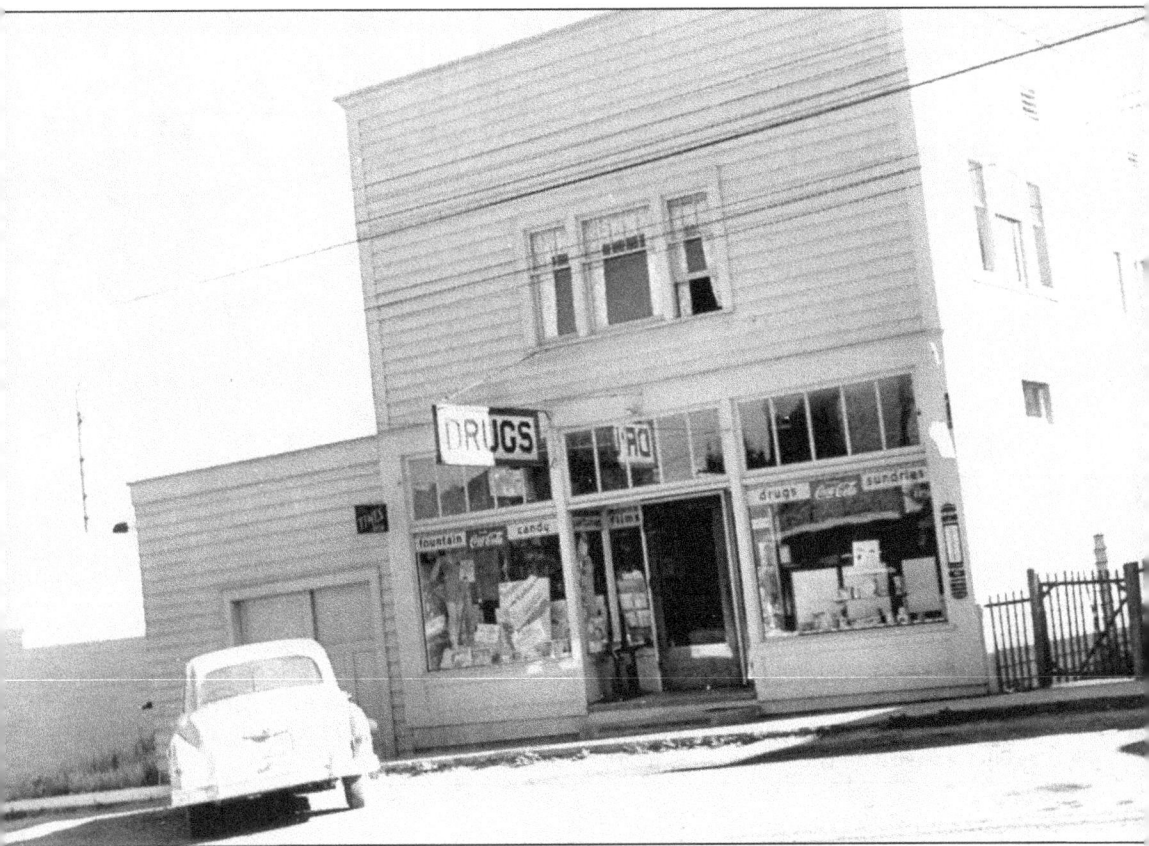

DRUGSTORE BUILT BY "DOC" MADSEN. A. C. Madsen moved to Alderwood Manor from the Green Lake neighborhood in Seattle and built this drugstore on the south side of the Alderwood Road in 1934. Ray Colby and his wife, Robbie, purchased the business in 1958. The Colbys lived in the apartment upstairs until they built a permanent home on Twenty-fourth Avenue West. Like Madsen and Dalrymple before him, Colby was available to fill emergency prescriptions at any hour.

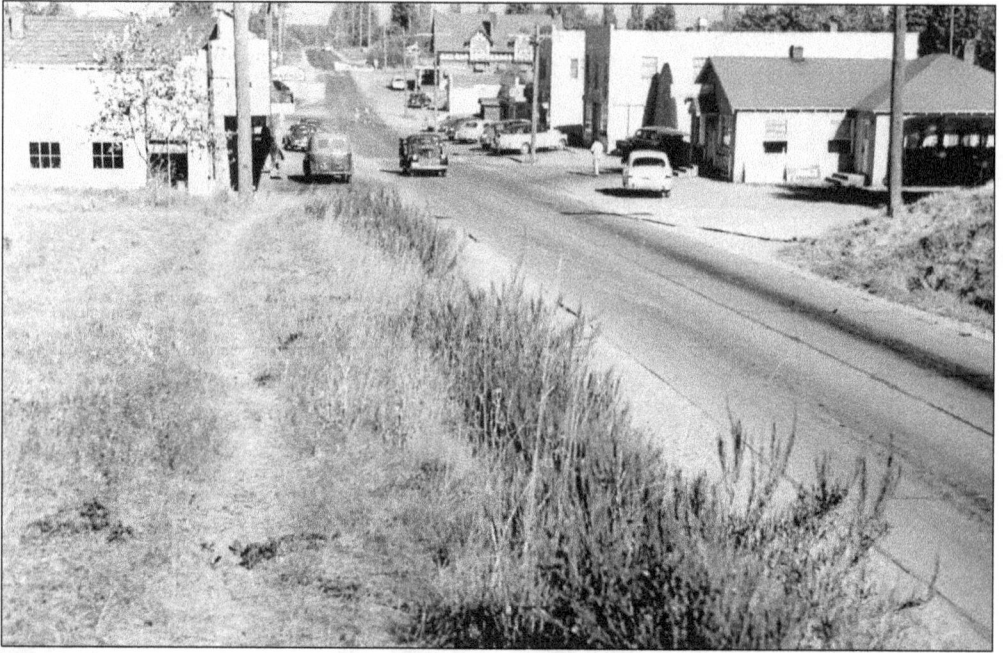

"MAIN STREET." Looking east from about Thirty-eighth Avenue West, the businesses on the right include a bakery, Dahlin's Red and White Store, the drugstore, and Alby Albright's barbershop in the small building just below the brick Tudor-style Alderwood Mercantile, c. 1950. Note the well-worn path on the left, used by nearby residents.

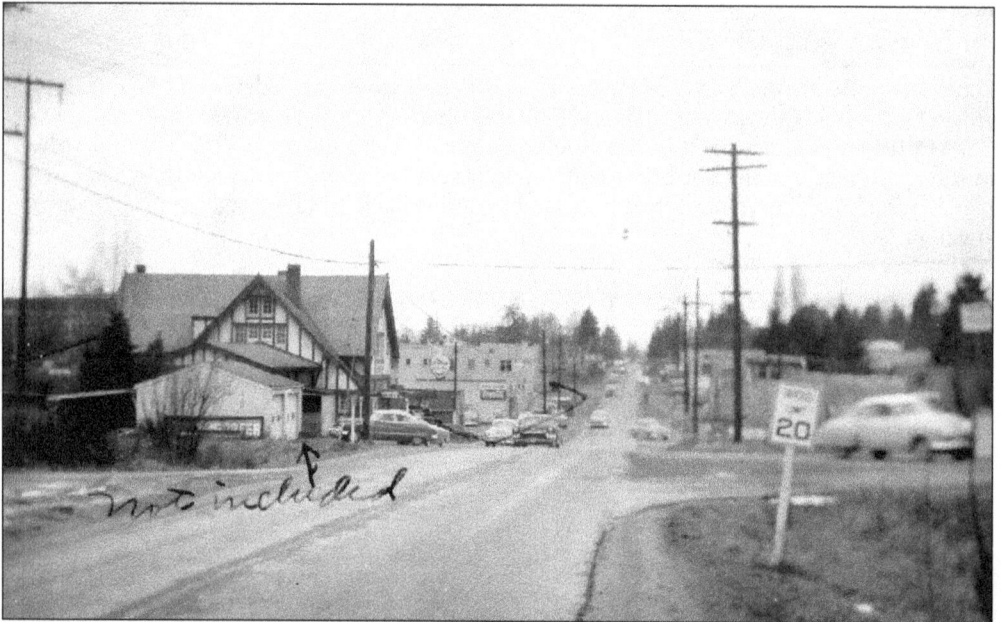

LOOKING WEST TOWARD LYNNWOOD. Although 196th Street is still a two-lane street in this c. 1960 view, note the increased traffic. The Alderwood Road was paved from this point to Highway 99 in 1933, and it had not changed much since then. This photograph was taken before the Alderwood Mercantile lost its front porch, and the drugstore was demolished as the street was widened to four lanes.

ALDERWOOD GRAIN COMPANY. In 1922, the Magnolia Milling Company in Ballard sent Bill Geltz out to open this business. Most people called it Bill Geltz's feed store, because they assumed he was the owner. He operated the store until he retired in 1959 and was one of the founders of the Alderwood Manor Youth Club, devoting many hours to working with young people in the community.

ALDERWOOD GRAIN COMPANY ON BEECH ROAD. Originally the building was on a spur of the interurban tracks, with supplies being delivered by the freight cars at night. It was located northeast of the Alderwood Road, between the Masonic temple and the Alderwood Community Church. Note that by 1950 the inventory had expanded to include tractors, hardware, and paint. Grain and coal were still sold.

CO-OP STORE, C. 1950. The Alderwood branch of the Washington Co-operative Farmers Association was constructed just across the tracks from the demonstration farm. Members could still fill up their trucks from the gas pump in the 1950s. The co-op was still in business as late as 1962; but by the 1980s, the building was occupied by a furniture warehouse.

CHARLEY OLSON'S COUNTRYSIDE DAIRY TRUCK. Charley milked a herd of 50 Jersey and Holsteins at his farm near the present intersection of 196th Street Southwest and Fifty-second Avenue West and delivered milk to customers in Cedar Valley, Alderwood, and Martha Lake from a horse-drawn wagon. In business for some 30 years, he later drove the route in this truck, c. 1930. Eventually he sold the route to an Everett dairy.

ELY'S GROCERY STORE.
Thomas and Katherine Ely built this store in the mid-1920s on their property, located about a mile east of Alderwood Manor, around the bend on Filbert Road. In the early 1950s, the store was used as a polling place. After elections were moved up to the school, some of the men who came to vote would remind Mrs. Ely that they once bought penny candy from her at the store.

DAHLIN BROTHERS GROCERY ON NORTH TRUNK ROAD NORTH. Arvid and David Dahlin's grocery store was located on the southwest corner of the present intersection of 164th Street Southwest and Thirty-sixth Avenue West, c. 1925. In those days, no one bothered to lock the door; if no one was home, the groceries were just left on the kitchen table. Arvid and his family lived in an apartment above the store.

AERIAL VIEW OF TOWN CENTER, 1953. Compare this image to the 1929 photograph at the beginning of this chapter. Although the demonstration farm disappeared some 20 years earlier, the former community hall, remodeled as a residence, is visible near the lower right corner. The Alderwood Community Church (center right) was not yet built in 1929. The brick Tudor-style Parker's store has not moved, but it became the Alderwood Mercantile in 1933. Also missing is the water tower behind the Puget Mill Real Estate office. Neither wells nor water towers were needed after the piped water system was put in during 1933 and 1934. The real estate office is gone, but the brick building, renamed Manor Hardware in 1947, remains across the street from the Masonic temple. (Courtesy Edmonds–South Snohomish County Historical Society.)

Six

THE AGE OF
THE AUTOMOBILE

VIEW OF PACIFIC HIGHWAY, LOOKING NORTH. Working north from the King Snohomish County line and south from the Everett city limits, paving crews met near the present 164th Street Southwest in Lynnwood. A celebration commemorating the completion of U.S. Highway 99 was held on October 25, 1927. The lone motorist did not have to contend with much traffic. As the highway neared completion, an Everett newspaper reported that the opening of the highway would mean law problems. Roadhouses, chicken dinner inns, and dance halls were expected to be erected along the new route, but the Snohomish County Sheriff warned that the south end of the county would not be permitted to become a "honky tonk."

EARLY DEVELOPMENT AT LAKE SERENE. The small building on Highway 99, center left, was the Puget Mill Company's Branch Office for the Shelby Additions, c. 1929. In the Shelby Addition, one-half-acre tracts with approximately 75 feet of water frontage were offered for sale at $1000. One-acre tracts of level ground, with beach privileges, in Shelby No. 2 could be purchased for $450.

INTERIOR OF LAKE SERENE STORE. Harry and Hildur Hopkins stocked auto supplies, such as anti-freeze in their store/service station, c. 1940. Mrs. Hopkins was the daughter of Agnes and Peter Wigen. Mr. Wigen was a salesman for the Puget Mill Co. in the 1940s. He built a large white house, overlooking Highway 99, for his family in 1927. It still stands at 4210 164th Street Southwest.

AERIAL VIEW OF HIGHWAY 99. Lake Serene is visible in the upper left of this photograph, and the Lake Serene Service Station and Store is at the center of this 1940 view. Follow the road at the lower right, to return to the Alderwood Manor Town Center. Several fir trees have grown up around the Puget Mill Company's Shelby Branch Office, which later was the Pope and Talbot Real Estate office.

SWIMMING IN MUD LAKE. Many Alderwood Manor old-timers remember swimming in Mud Lake before it became Lake Serene. Around 1925, Jean Thomson Holt snapped this picture of her brothers, sisters, and friends.

KEELER'S KORNER, BETWEEN SEATTLE AND EVERETT. Keeler's Korner, now on the National Register of Historic Places, has been a local landmark since it was built, shortly after the ribbon cutting ceremony which opened Highway 99 was held at this intersection (now 164th Street Southwest) on October 25, 1927.

LOOP SERVICE ON THE WEST SIDE OF 99. Horace Nelson had two telephones in his station, which was a few blocks south of Keeler's Korner at the present 168th Street Southwest intersection. One was for calls to Alderwood Manor; the other for calls to Edmonds. The west side of Highway 99 was in the Edmonds telephone service area, while the east side was in Alderwood Manor. As late as 1950, calls between Alderwood and Edmonds were long distance.

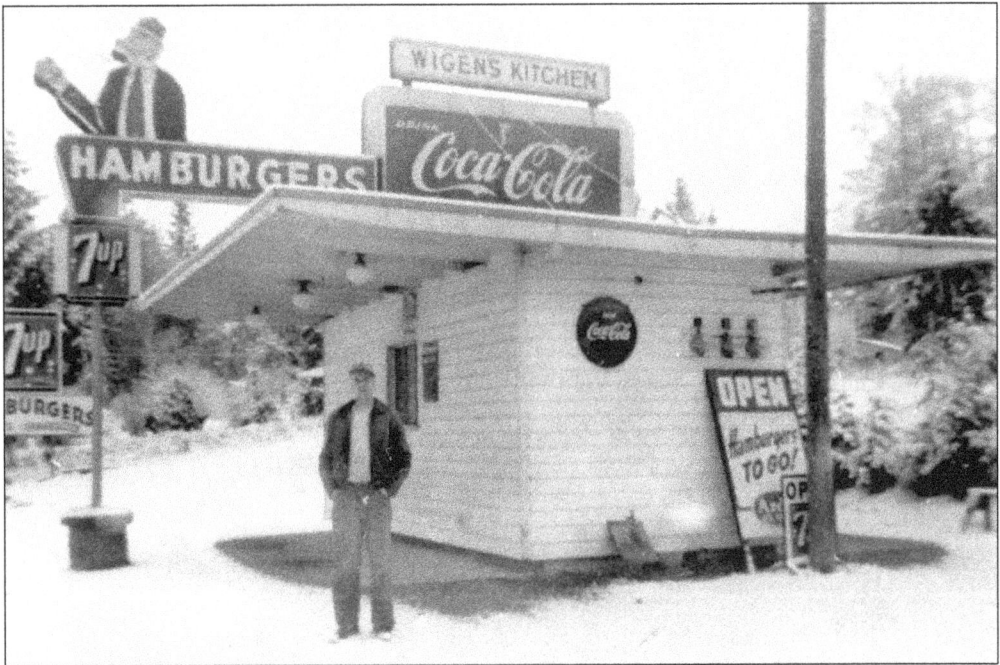

POPULAR DRIVE-THROUGH ON 99. Clarence Wigen stands in front of Wigen's Kitchen, which many people called "Wimpy's" because they were so impressed with the image of the cartoon character on the neon sign.

PINE CONE CAFÉ. Highway 99 cut the Gunderson property in half. Two decades later, their son Marvin built this café on the east side of Highway 99 across from the site of his parents' farmhouse. A large chain grocery store has now replaced the popular café, which was north of 176th Street Southwest.

INTERIOR OF PINE CONE. Customers still remember the good hamburgers and pie served at the lunch counter. Perhaps the woman on the left is enjoying one of their Green River floats, c. 1945.

SNO-KING DRIVE-IN THEATRE SITE. Across the highway from the Pine Cone, the second outdoor theatre built in Washington State opened on June 1, 1948. *The Tycoon,* starring John Wayne and Loraine Day, played on the first night, and tickets were 65¢. Owned by C. J. and Carmelita Rockey, the Sno-King was built for 500 cars and later expanded to 750. It closed in 1986. A large thrift store now occupies the site.

COX CANDY BOX. Delectable chocolates were made and sold here on the southwest corner of the intersection of 176th Street Southwest. In this August 1948 photograph, construction appears to be underway on one of the strip malls that lined the highway over the next few years.

SOUTH SNOHOMISH COUNTY ROADHOUSE. Rubenak's offered dining, dancing, and, if rumors are to be believed, illegal beverages, c. 1930. Throughout the 1940s, people came from as far as Vancouver, British Columbia, to dance to the live music. It was located on the east side of the highway near the present 188th Street Southwest.

BILLBOARD IN LYNNWOOD BUSINESS DISTRICT. Lew Williams parked his truck near this billboard, erected near Highway 99 at the Alderwood Crossroad, to advertise his business, Evergreen Decorators which was about a mile and a half east of Lynnwood, at the Alderwood Town Center.

ALBRIGHT'S CAFÉ AT ALDERWOOD CROSSROAD. Albion (Alby) Albright and his wife, Ann, operated this café from 1936 until 1939, when the rent was raised from $40 to $125 per month. After the war, Albright opened a barbershop in Alderwood Manor and served over 40 years as a commissioner for Fire District 1.

FIRST LYNNWOOD BUSINESS. In 1937, Carl O'Beirn, a Seattle realtor, platted an 18-acre tract on the southeast corner of the present intersection of 196th Street Southwest and Highway 99, naming it Lynnwood. He encouraged Pete Fulton, who bought the first lot to name his business Lynnwood Lumber. Other businesses followed suit, and the Lynnwood Business District was established.

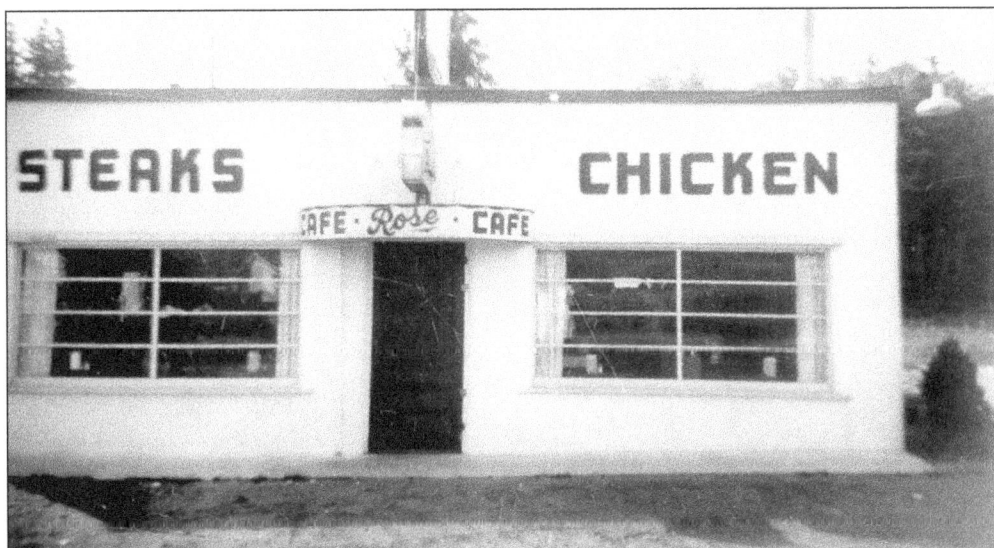

ROSE CAFÉ. This café was built because Rose Keltner, on a ride in the country, put $10 down on property for sale on the west side of Highway 99, about half a mile south of the Alderwood Crossroad. The Rose Café was located on the southwest corner of the present intersection of 202nd and Highway 99, c. 1945. New owners changed the name to the Chicken Roost; it is now an accounting office.

On U.S.99 - 14 Mi. N.of Seattle..13 Mi.S.of Everett

ROSE MOTEL – A FAMILY MOTEL – PH. GREENWOOD 2447 – LYNWOOD, WA

ROSE MOTEL UNITS WITH EFFICIENCY KITCHENS. In 1951, Maynard and Rose Keltner built this modern motel on the property they bought for $1,400. This postcard shows the Rose to be one of the nicer motels on Highway 99 in the 1950s. It was demolished in 2004 to make room for a Lexus dealership.

Seven

DAYS OF PROGRESS

FIRST LYNNWOOD DAYS OF PROGRESS FESTIVAL PARADE. A festival, which became an annual event, started as a joint fund-raising project of the Lynnwood Commercial Club and the Lynnwood Community Club to raise money for a park. Pictured is Marie Tutmark of Alderwood Manor, sporting an elegant mink stole perhaps made from animals raised on her brother-in-law Pete Tutmark's mink ranch. Mrs. Tutmark owned Marie's Floral Shop at 19201 Park Way in Lynnwood. The unidentified driver has parked the official car on the west side of the present intersection of 196th Street Southwest and Highway 99, considered by some to be the historic center of Lynnwood. The building on the left is a hardware store owned by Verhey and Sons. The first Days of Progress festival was held in 1951 and included events such as a street dance and a baby photograph contest. By 1959 (the year Lynnwood was incorporated), the Days of Progress festival had been replaced by the more up-to-date Lynn-O-Rama, which continued for many years.

GROUND BROKEN FOR DEVELOPMENT IN LYNNWOOD. Once Pete Fulton built the Lynnwood Lumber Company, the business district developed rapidly. Frank Lockhow built a cabinet shop across the highway and named it the Lynnwood Cabinet Shop. Arie Vehrey and his sons James and John bartered bulldozer work for a tract in the Lynnwood Plat in 1939 and built a feed store they called Lynnwood Feeder Supply. (Courtesy City of Lynnwood.)

CENTER OF SOUTH SNOHOMISH COUNTY. Appropriately, Lynnwood Junior High School appears at the center of this 1953 photograph. This first junior high school in South Snohomish County was at the center of School District 15. Highway 99 is visible, cutting diagonally from top right to center left. The two-lane Alderwood Road, (196th Street Southwest), is nearly invisible as it curves around Scriber Lake (lower right). (Courtesy City of Lynnwood.)

FOURTH LARGEST CITY IN COUNTY. On April 14, 1959, Lynnwood incorporated. Six months later, they purchased this brick residence on Fifty-second Avenue West for a city hall and jail, pictured here in 1964. The first city council meetings were held in the community room of the Lynnwood Junior High School, pictured on the hill above the city hall. (Courtesy City of Lynnwood.)

LONG-STANDING NURSERY. Wight's Nursery offered rock salt and roses for sale in the winter of 1964. It still stands at 5026 196th Street Southwest but has expanded a great deal and has been joined by a number of neighboring businesses. (Courtesy Edmonds–South Snohomish County Historical Society.)

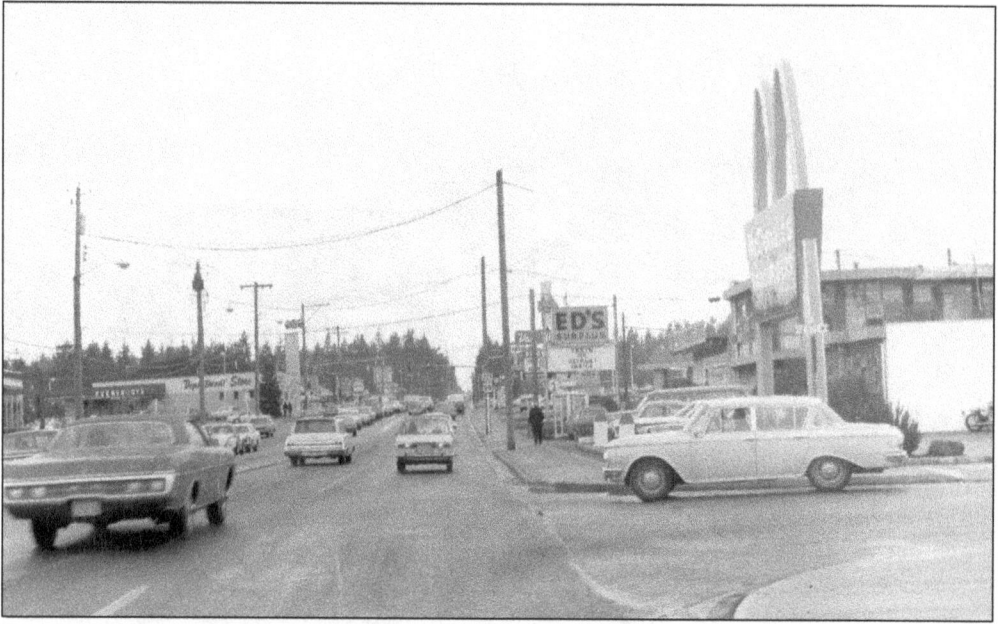

LYNNWOOD SHOPPING CENTER. Everybody's Department Store, on the left, is at the northwest corner of the Lynnwood Shopping Center, viewed looking west from the intersection of 58th Avenue West and 196th Street Southwest, c. 1964. McDonalds has since moved to several different locations in the city, but Ed's Surplus remains. (Courtesy City of Lynnwood.)

ALDERWOOD SHOPPING CENTER. Two miles east of the Lynnwood Shopping Center, Alderwood Manor had a new Shop N Save next to a new Post Office located in the building on the right, c. 1964. In 2005, a video store that occupied the former post office was demolished to make way for the Lynnwood Convention Center. In the foreground is the lot where the Alderwood Manor School stood for 70 years. (Courtesy Edmonds–South Snohomish County Historical Society.)

PROGRESS BYPASSES MANOR HARDWARE. This 75-year-old building was still open for business in 1992. Construction of a new freeway entrance ramp, however, routed traffic behind the building, leaving it to face a mere remnant of 36th Avenue West. Now it stands vacant in the shadow of the Lynnwood Convention Center. The structure on the right is a motel. Listed on Lynnwood's Historic Landmarks Register in 2005, Manor Hardware awaits renovation.

FREEWAY CONSTRUCTION DISPLACES YOUTH CLUB. In 1948, the school board gave Alderwood Manor Youth Club volunteers permission to erect an army surplus building, purchased for $950 on the west end of Alderwood Elementary School's playground. In 1958, members of the youth club were notified that freeway construction would bisect their property. In this c. 1962 photograph, construction is underway just southeast of the Alderwood Manor Town Center.

AERIAL VIEW OF I-5 UNDER CONSTRUCTION. This view looks north towards Lynnwood and Alderwood Manor from a position over Lake Ballinger, near the King County border. The freeway, on the right, cuts a much broader swath than Highway 99, which is the narrow stripe near the left border of the photograph. The oval field near Highway 99, a little past the center of the photograph, marks Lynnwood Junior High School. Nearby, the old Alderwood Road (196th Street Southwest) may be seen, at the point where it curves past Scriber Lake. At the point where the freeway curves into the right border of the photograph, Exit 181 onto Forty-fourth Avenue West is under construction, c. 1962. (Courtesy City of Lynnwood.)

Eight

SPIRIT OF COMMUNITY

SPRUCING UP MASONIC TEMPLE. Built by members of the Robert Burns Masonic Lodge, in 1921, the Masonic temple served the community as well. Within two years, the social hall could no longer accommodate all of the settlers for a meeting, but the auditorium in the temple could comfortably seat nearly 1,000 people. In addition to being used as a public meeting hall, it served as a theatre for moving picture matinees as well as benefit performances for local groups such as the Ladies Library Club. Pictured are community volunteers sprucing up the grounds in 1936. Bill Geltz has brought tools and supplies in the Alderwood Grain Company truck. Today there is a strip mall replacing the house in the background, which was later owned by John Burke, the schoolteacher. The Masonic temple now serves as a church for a Vietnamese congregation.

WILLIAM MORRICE FURNISHED CORNERSTONE. The cornerstone for the Robert Burns Masonic Lodge was salvaged from a building that had been razed in Seattle. Pictured in his barn, where the cornerstone was carved, is William Morrice, who had been a Mason in his native Scotland.

RESTING ON THE STEPS OF MASONIC TEMPLE. With the afternoon's work accomplished, volunteers relax. Bill Geltz heads back to the feed store with the Alderwood Grain Company truck.

MEMBERS OF ROBERT BURNS MASONIC LODGE. Pictured, from left to right, are (first row) Ernie Forstell, Harry Hill, unidentified, Bob Ewing, Bert Shipley, William Birt, and unidentified; (second row) unidentified, Alby Albright, Ben Johnson, Art Beam, and Jack Beam. (Photograph by Harry Tutmark.)

The Mishaps of Minerva

A FARCE IN TWO ACTS

By Bertha Currier Porter

—Produced By—

ALDERWOOD MANOR CHRISTIAN ENDEAVOR

CAST OF CHARACTERS

MORTIMER J. STERLING, an easy-going
business man ....Edward Bedier
VICTOR BROWN, a young doctor, friend of
the family and especially of Minerva.......Harry Cook
HARRY STEVENSON, a "cub" reporter,
attentive to Clara ....Douglas McClane
BARNES, the butler ....Earl Martin
MIKE SHANNON, a very new policeman
....................................Charles Thompson
MRS. LYDIA STERLING, domestic and
quiet ....Viola Rudd
MINERVA STERLING, willing to oblige..Dorothy Chase
CLARA STERLING, her younger sister....Posey Miller
MOLLY, the maid ....Ruth Morrice
BELLE BRANTLEY, reporter for "The
Screamer" ....Mrs. Chas. Thompson
MRS. WRIGHT, a club woman...........Elinore Anderson
MISS PALMER, a philanthropic worker
..................................Ethel Richardson
MRS. JENNIE VAN DEUSEN SPUYKER, a personage

Under the direction of
MRS. S. J. BARNEY,

Masonic Temple, Friday, June 16

At 8:00 o'clock P. M.

General Admission 35c   Children Under 12 years 20c

Reserved Seats 50c—on sale at Alderwood Main Store

Ice cream cone given free by Mr. Horowitz to every

purchaser of a reserved seat ticket.

Tribune-Review Print, Edmonds, Wn.

PLAYBILL FROM BENEFIT PERFORMANCE. The Christian Endeavor youth group of the Alderwood
Manor Church produced and performed this play in 1922. They made arrangements for Mr.
Horowitz, the owner of the Main Store, to sell reserved seats for 50¢, and he generously provided
a free ice cream cone for anyone who purchased a ticket at the store. Sunday-school classes met
in the Masonic temple before the church was built, so members of the cast would have to be sure
all the chairs were back in place by Sunday morning.

WHANG DOODLE QUARTET BY MASONIC TEMPLE. Pictured *c.* 1923, from left to right, are Harry Cook, Douglas McClane, Art Coyne, and Ed Bedier.

PAINTING ALDERWOOD MANOR COMMUNITY CHURCH. The truck is Lew Williams' 1936 Ford. He was the owner of Evergreen Decorators, located just down the street in the Post Office Building. Undoubtedly he is one of the volunteers, *c.* 1939.

COUNTRYSIDE SINGERS IN CONCERT. The Countryside Singers formed in the 1950s from a group of Alderwood Manor residents who loved to sing. Led by local school music teacher Bob Burton, the group was still singing in the 1960s.

TRINITY LUTHERAN CHURCH IN LYNNWOOD. Mrs. Eugene Wilcox surveyed the neighborhood around the Alderwood Crossroad in 1940 and found they were interested in forming a church. The first services were held at the Wilcox home, and in 1946, a permanent brick building was dedicated at 6215 196th Street Southwest. The congregation outgrew the building and built another larger sanctuary that was destroyed in an arson fire in 1992. The congregation now meets in an impressive 46,000-square-foot building at the same location. (Courtesy Trinity Lutheran Church.)

CEDAR VALLEY GRANGE BUILDING'S ORIGINAL LOCATION. Organized as the Halls Lake Grange in 1909, their first building was near the interurban tracks at about 212th Street. The name was changed to Cedar Valley in 1927, and by the 1930s, there were 150 members on the rolls. In 1948, the building was moved to its present site on Fifty-second Avenue West, near 205th Street Southwest, and remodeled.

CEDAR VALLEY GRANGE'S ACTIVE JUVENILE GRANGE. Pictured are the officers of the Cedar Valley Junior Grange, c. 1944. From left to right, they are (first row) Mary Shipley, Pat Lewis, Jean Ann Smith, Clarette LeBlanc, Donna Allen, and Teresa Neal; (second row) Lorna Wilcox, Adena Cox, Beth Hughes, Barbara Campbell, Drusilla Thompson, Joyce Vailar, and assistant advisor Jack Johnson.

LIBRARY BUILT BY LADIES LIBRARY CLUB. Mrs. Engler, the librarian, was photographed by one of her young patrons, *c.* 1939. In 1941, this building was destroyed by fire, but the Puget Mill Company donated the land where the library stood, and the insurance money was used to purchase another house and move it onto the lot at 16016 Lake Road (Thirty-sixth Avenue West). In 1945, it became the first branch of the Snohomish County Library system.

LADIES LIBRARY CLUB PICNIC. Members of the Community Library Club gathered for a picnic in 1928. Pictured, from left to right, are Mrs. Henry Engler, Mrs. Al Peterson (holding little girl), Mrs. Lew Williams (holding her baby Bob), Molly Peterson, and Lewis Williams. The lady in the black dress, standing on the right, is Lillian Keeler, the first librarian. The Alderwood Manor Library Club was incorporated in 1921.

BOY SCOUT TROOP 49 HALL. Members of Troop 49 are working on their hall located at 19500 Thirty-sixth Avenue West, just north of the Post Office Building, *c.* 1936. As usual, Bill Geltz has volunteered to help with the Alderwood Grain Company truck.

TROOP 49 TRAILER AT WASHINGTON STATE CAPITAL. The boys built a trailer and set out on a trip to Mexico, in 1947, traveling through Washington, Oregon, and California. Jack and Ruth Allen pulled the trailer with their 1939 Ford.

ALDERWOOD YOUTH CLUB RODEO. Often youth club events were held in this stadium, which was built in 1936 as a WPA project. The playfield was located on property east of the interurban tracks. Originally a bridge was built across the tracks so that students could walk to the playfields without being hit by a train. The original youth club building was on the west side of the playfield.

PEGASUS PATROL DRILL TEAM IN PLAY DAY PARADE. This horse organization was started in 1946 to train youngsters in horsemanship. Soon affiliated with the Alderwood Manor Youth Club, and later a 4-H chapter, the group was active through the 1960s. In this 1950 view, the horses are headed west on 196th Street Southwest, approaching Thirty-seventh Avenue West. The Alderwood Grain Company is the building on the far right.

A M Y C

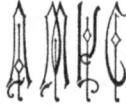

Alderwood Manor Youth Club

HONORARY DEED

The Grantee, *the Alderwood Manor Youth Club, Incorporated, a non-profit Washington corporation, acknowledges receipt of the sum of_____ dollars, from the grantor _____*

Said sum being donated by the grantor for the purchase by the grantee herein of_____ square yards, a portion of that certain real property located in the County of Snohomish, State of Washington, more particularly described as follows, to-wit:

S ½ of the NW ¼ of the NE ¼ of the NW¼ of Sec. 23 T 27N R 4 E WM

The grantor herein gives said money and any and all rights to any personal and or real property acquired thereby to the grantee herein for the uses and purposes as set forth in the by-laws of the grantee corporation and for the benefits derived by the grantor and his friends, neighbors and the youth of South Snohomish County.

In witness whereof the undersigned sign and affix their seal this_____ day of_____19___

_____
President

_____
Treasurer

"YARDS FOR YOUTH" CAMPAIGN. To raise money for a new building, the members of the Youth Club sold honorary deeds for square yards of the property for $1. Interest-bearing bonds were delivered to the youth club in a packsack. A total of $14,000 was raised. When the first interest checks were sent to investors, many were returned with notes such as, "the youth club needs it more than I do." Construction of the new hall began in May 1962. Volunteers erected cement block walls for the 80-by-44-foot main section in one day. Six months later, the building was complete. Valued at over $60,000, the hall was built for only $13,000.

CHRISTIAN ENDEAVOR BOAT TRIP. The youth group sponsored by the Alderwood Manor Community Church enjoyed a boat trip in the early 1920s. Pictured, from left to right, are (first row) Dorothy McClane, Ruth Morrice, Eloa Harper, Shirley Chase, and Frances Reid; (second row) Ada Spade, an unidentified chicken expert from Petaluma, and Jenn Chase.

BASEBALL TEAM. Local merchants sponsored a baseball team, *c.* 1940. Home games were played on the school ball field. Pictured, from left to right, are (first row) Archie Johnson, Winston Norgar, Ellsworth Wilcox, Bill Birt, Morgan Bartlett, and Knox Bellingham; batboy Rudy Johnson and manager Norm Johnson (center); (second row) Frank Hoff, Chuck Johnson, Johnny Johnson, Don Day, Babe Bucklin, Otto Lambe, ? Fredrickson, and Kenny Wilcox.

ALDERWOOD INTRAMURAL BASKETBALL TEAM. There was quite a rivalry between the Alderwood boys and the Edmonds boys at Edmonds High School. But in 1950, the Alderwood boys were the champs. Pictured, from left to right, are (first row) Stathos, Stan Echelbarger, and Arne Nelson; (second row) Gill Kaslaw, Larry Wooley, DeWayne Lallaz, Gene Thomas, Karl Stadler, and Kirt ?.

ALDERWOOD GIRLS DRILL TEAM. American Legion Post No. 90 sponsored the drill team shown here in 1940. Pictured, from left to right, are Chickie Johnson, Astrid Ellingson, Lorna Swanson, Ragna Ellingson, Shirley Mauser, Irene Johnson, Dorothy Stadler, Eugenie King, Betty Denby, Florence Farr, Delores Flatum, Mary Thompson, Jean Brampton, Drusilla Thompson, Joanne Peterson, Ardelle Wilcox, Marjorie Wilson, and Lila Ewing. In front are Walt Jones and little Yvonne Henderson.

ALDERWOOD PLAY DAYS PARADE, 1955. In 1949, the Alderwood Manor Youth Club organized a "Community Day" with the support of local merchants. Events included a parade, a mounted polo game played with broomsticks and a beach ball, a barbecue dinner, and two ball games. The following year, the name was changed to Play Day, and in 1951, merchants began providing ribbons for competitive events. In 1952, a second day was added and the event became "Play Days."

PLAY DAY PARADE, 1955. Participants in the 1955 parade included a horse-drawn wagon; decorated vehicles, including one from Orner's Men and Boy's Shop in Lynwood; the always-popular Pegasus Patrol; and a float with the theme "A Prayer for Peace." Businesses in the building on the north side of 196th Street Southwest included a meat market, Alderwood Radio Service, and Henry's Garage, which was on the northwest corner of Thirty-seventh Avenue West and 196th Street.

ALDERWOOD MANOR STATION NO. 2. Many of the Alderwood Manor firemen were merchants. When the siren atop the building sounded the alert, they left their shops and rushed to the fire station. Pictured, from left to right, are (first row) Lee Hollowell, Bill Birt, Ralph Roper, unidentified, Lew Silver, and Skeet Tutmark; (second row) unidentified, Herman Wickers, Virgil Schoentrup, Larry Miller, and Lew Williams. The Alderwood Community Library occupied a room in this building.

FIRE DISTRICT 1 STATION AT LAKE SERENE. Fire Station No. 3 was built in 1951 to serve the area north of Alderwood Manor. The volunteer firemen pictured, from left to right, are Ald Bye, unidentified, unidentified, Art Kessler, unidentified, unidentified, Gary Thomaier, John Havlicek, Gus Wigen, and unidentified.

FIRE PREVENTION WEEK, 1955. In 1938, the Seattle Heights Community Club bought a 1926 Reo fire engine from the City of Edmonds. This was the beginning of Snohomish County Fire District 1. As the community grew so did the needs of the fire department. Pictured here is the entire fleet of Fire District 1 in 1955, including the Reo (on the far right). Although it is no longer in use, the fire department still owns the Reo.

PROMOTING FIRE SAFETY AT LYNNWOOD SHOPPING CENTER. In 1959, the community of Alderwood Manor and the City of Lynwood still relied on a volunteer fire department. As part of fire prevention week, fireman Jim Bell and Karl Stadler volunteered to provide information on fire safety to residents by handing out brochures and answering questions at the entrance to the Thriftway Grocery.

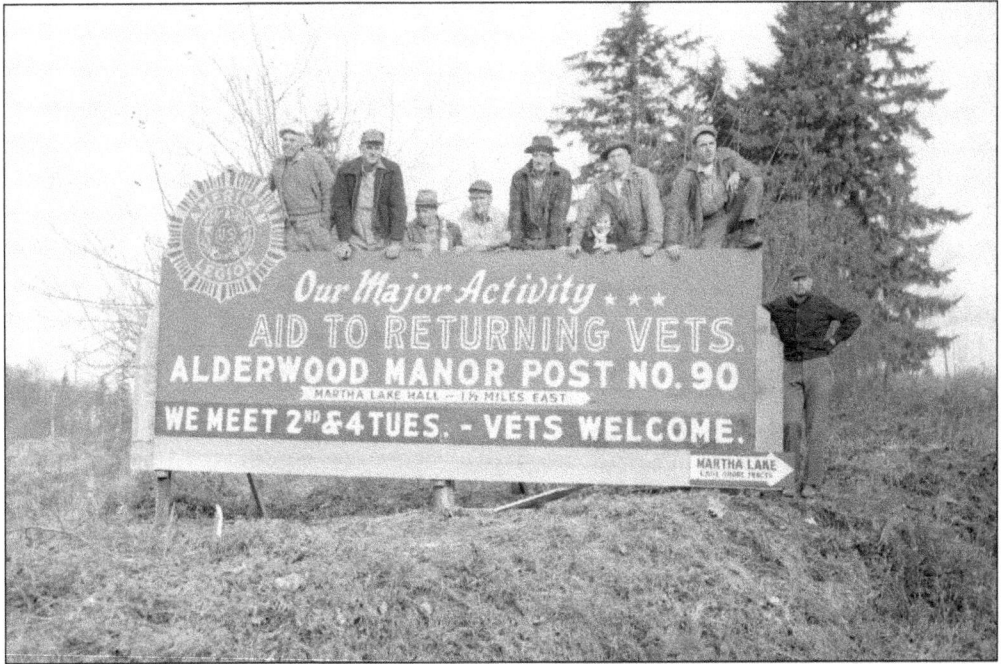

AMERICAN LEGION POST NO. 90 BILLBOARD. Members of American Legion Post No. 90 erected a billboard on Martha Lake Road inviting veterans to attend their meetings at the Martha Lake Community Club, c. 1945. Originally, they planned to build a Legion Hall at the Alderwood Town Center, however, after the war; the property was donated for the Alderwood Manor Fire Station which was built in 1950.

WAR MEMORIAL DEDICATED. Members of VFW Post 1040 erected this memorial dedicated to those of School District 15 who gave their lives for their country in the First and Second World Wars on the east side of Highway 99 at 52nd Avenue, West, c. 1946. Later moved to the grounds of Lynnwood Junior High School, its present location is in front of the Edmonds Historical Museum.

"In the Swim" at Martha Lake. In the 1920s, the Tutmark cousins walked from nearby Tutmark Hill to swim in Martha Lake. The lake continued to be popular with the young swimmers, such as the youngsters pictured here in the 1940s, although by then there was a small charge. The Red Cross also offered swimming lessons at Martha Lake in the 1940s.

Martha Lake Resort. In 1934, a model summer resort at Martha Lake was operated by Mr. and Mrs. T. E. Ferling and their daughter, Mrs. Ann Langley. They employed Lloyd Maneval and Robert Rogers, Red Cross–certified lifeguards, to assure the safety of the patrons. Large community kitchens; free, split firewood; tables, cabins; bath houses, and boats for hire were also available for a small admission fee.

Nine

FREEWAY TO HERITAGE PARK

PRESERVING HERITAGE IN A TIME OF PROGRESS. To bring the historic community of Alderwood Manor back to life, the City of Lynnwood opened Heritage Park in May 2004. The park is located just west of the original site of the Alderwood Demonstration Farm. Pictured cutting the ribbon for the new park are Mayor Mike McKinnon and Betty Wickers Gruwell. Betty is the daughter of Herman and Anita Wickers, who operated the Alderwood Mercantile for more than 30 years. Holding the ribbon are Mary Humble Wickstrom (on the left) and Janice Humble Tutmark, whose childhood home still stands on the grounds of the park. Heritage Park is located at 19921 Poplar Way in Lynnwood. (Courtesy City of Lynnwood.)

ALDERWOOD MANOR HERITAGE COTTAGE. The Alderwood Manor Heritage Association (AMHA) has reconstructed the superintendent's cottage, originally built on the demonstration farm c. 1917. Located at Heritage Park, the association's resource center is open to the public. Visitors can see interpretive displays and view the Association's collection of photographs, newspapers, manuscripts, and oral histories. The AMHA also offers regular programs on the history of the area.

HUMBLE HOUSE. This residence still stands where it was originally built in 1919. It was not included in the 2.54 acres of property sold by the family to the City of Lynnwood in 1999 because it had earlier been purchased by a developer and might have become a strip mall. The owner, however, decided to sell it to the city for inclusion in Heritage Park, and it was named for the Humble family, who moved into it in 1934. Today it is home to the Sno-Isle Genealogical Society's Library and Resource Center. (Courtesy City of Lynnwood.)

INTERURBAN CAR 55. This 1909, single-ended wooden electric rail car served the community of Alderwood Manor on the Seattle–Everett Interurban line from 1910 to 1939. Purchased by the City of Lynnwood in 1993 from the Northwest Railway Museum, where it was found deteriorating amongst the weeds, the car was restored in 1995 as a static display at Heritage Park. Today visitors can climb aboard historic Car 55 during scheduled tours and learn about the interurban. (Courtesy City of Lynnwood.)

WICKERS BUILDING. Built in 1919 by the Puget Mill Company as the Main Store, the Wickers Building served the community for 75 years as a grocery store. In later years, it was an appliance repair and parts store. To save the historic building from the I-5 freeway construction project, the City of Lynwood relocated it to Heritage Park, where it has been restored. It is now home to the South Snohomish County Visitor Information Center. The city has received several awards for the restoration project. (Courtesy City of Lynnwood.)

WATER TOWER. This water tower was located at the original Alderwood demonstration farm and was unique in its day, as its pump was powered by electricity. It has been relocated to the park and is slated for restoration in 2006. It will then be opened to the public with programs on the agricultural heritage of the community. (Courtesy City of Lynnwood.)

HERITAGE PARK. In 1997, when three historic structures were threatened with demolition for the I-5 freeway interchange, the concept of Heritage Park was created. In 1999, the city purchased a three-acre park site for relocation of these historical structures. In May 2004, the park opened to give local residents and visitors a look back at the unique history of the community of Alderwood Manor. (Courtesy City of Lynnwood.)

CHICKENS RETURN. Alderwood Manor was once a top egg-producing region in the United States. Today, if you ask people who grew up in Alderwood Manor, they will tell you it was a great place to be a child. The sculpture at Heritage Park by Louise McDowell depicts the chickens that were a central part of the community and the children who experienced the "new life of the land" at Alderwood Manor Washington.

Visit us at
arcadiapublishing.com

www.ingramcontent.com/pod-product-compliance
Lightning Source LLC
Chambersburg PA
CBHW080547110426
42813CB00006B/1237